AMERICAN POET

VOL. 1

John T. Eber Sr.
MANAGING EDITOR

A publication of

Eber & Wein Publishing

Pennsylvania

American Poet: Vol. 1
Copyright © 2016 by Eber & Wein Publishing as a compilation.

Rights to individual poems reside with the artist themselves. This collection of poetry contains works submitted to the publisher by individual authors who confirm that the work is their original creation. Based upon the author's confirmations and to that of the Publisher's actual knowledge, these poems were written by the listed poets. Eber & Wein, Inc. does not guarantee or assume responsibility for verifying the authorship of each work.

The views expressed within certain poems contained in this anthology do not necessarily reflect the views of the editors or staff of Eber & Wein Publishing.

All rights reserved under the International and Pan-American copyright conventions. No part of this book may be reproduced, stored in a retrieval system, or transmitted in any form, electronic, mechanical, or by other means, without written permission of the publisher. Address all inquires to Rachel Eber, 50 E. High St., New Freedom, PA 17349.

Library of Congress
Cataloging in Publication Data

ISBN 978-1-60880-531-0

Proudly manufactured in the United States of America by

Eber & Wein Publishing
Pennsylvania

Sweet Lady, Awake! A Serenade

Sweet lady awake, from your slumbers awake,
Weird beings we come o'er hill and through brake
To sing you a song in the stillness of night
Oh, read you our riddle fair lady aright?
We are sent by the one whose found heart is your own,
Who mourns in thy absence and sighs all alone.
Alas, he is distant—but tho' far, far away,
He thinks of you, Lady, by night and by day.
Sweet lady awake, sweet lady awake!
His hearth, altho' lonely, is bright with your fame,
And therefore we breathe not the breath of his name.
For oh! if your dreams have response in your tone,
Long since have you known it as well as your own.
We are things of the sea, of the earth, and the air,
But ere you again to your pillow repair,
Entrust us to say you gave ear to our strain,
And were he the minstrel you would listen again.
Sweet lady awake, sweet lady awake!

—President John Tyler (1843)

Presidents' Day

Presidents' Day is
A yearly holiday where we
Honor every single president:

From George Washington,
The father of our country,
To Abraham Lincoln,

Who freed the slaves, to
John Kennedy who was shot
In the head while riding,

To George W. Bush,
Who prayed for families
During the 9-11 attack,

To Barack Obama,
The first black president that
Defeated Saddam Hussein, so

Let's give a
Standing ovation for these men,
We salute you all.

Jylan Ross
Lexington, KY

One Nation, Under God

Our country is the home we treasure
Full of freedom and diversity
But this age shows signs of changing
Filled with decay and adversity

America used to stand for strength
States united in solid alliance
The land of opportunity
Built on hope and self-reliance

Jesus Christ is the foundation
The solid *rock* on which we should stand
The true reliability of God
Makes everything else feel like sand

What America needs is rescue
From its state of disrepair
Jesus Christ is the great healer
Whose power is strong and fair

A house divided is not a home
And conflict tears people apart
We need to be one nation *under God*
To give America a renewed start

Amy Pratt
Marion, IA

Girl in a Picture

Light, free, nature flowers
A peaceful sense, of well being
As the water ebbs and flows,
  by a quiet creek
Sunlight slips away peaceful,
  and meek
You can almost feel the breeze,
  so warm and sweet
Water lapped on gray rocks
Ducks swim near the dock
A girl any minute going to
Lift her fan and use it
Old and very rustic
You can almost feel how,
  warm it is
The way she's got her
  head back
And yes, she's too warm
Any minute she's going,
  to fan her face and neck

Connie R. Holt
Waynesboro, TN

Ilise Lost: To Ilise White

On the anniversary
Of your death,
Cotton ball clouds drift
Across warm, azure sky.
A blizzard comes tomorrow,
But today is warm
And the sky is azure,
So even though
You were lost a year ago,
The sky is warm and azure,
While clouds and angels
Drift across
The warm, azure sky.

Richard Stepsay
Aurora, CO

Get Connected!

The whole world's mysteriously intoxicated with the grooviest
   technology
But why so many hoodwinked to tossing away sound theology?
Why have those playthings become more precious than people?
While the aging stalwart church pillars cling anchored to the solid
   rock, bellowing out their praises beneath that spiraling steeple
Criminal activity fearfully accelerates everywhere every day
Newscasters spiel off—rattling hourly horror happenings
   without delay
Our chaotic world's a seething pressure cooker, sizzling daily from
   bad to worse
While an illusive shadow slyly floats around loading a shiny hearse
Distressed races and ideologies clash in the street
When suddenly, flashing patrol cars zip right past my feet
O Lord above, save me from this
And fly me upward into your glorious heavenly bliss!
Meanwhile, global innovation technology forever expands, soars
   and scores
While humanity spills red and suffers through endless wars
I guess clever technology by itself is really okay
But our Lord's salvation surely delivers all those who are prone
   to pray

William H. Shuttleworth
Jacksonville, FL

Once in a while a poetic effort of mine will blossom out like a beautiful flower. But most often I sweat and strain like a cowboy roping and wrestling a steer to the ground. Nevertheless, I've enjoyed unexpected awards and ventures of various kinds over my two and a half decades of poetic writing. "Never made enough money from it to buy even one pair of shoelaces," as William Wordsworth put it. Regardless, poetry still finds me digging deeply into the depths of my mind and soul to find something worthy of sharing with others, while at the same time bringing honor and glory to God. So, here once again is my latest unveiling, now appearing on a page of this prestigious anthology.

American Poet

Sanity Lost

I lost it
I lost it
Some place
Some time ago
I had it here
Oh so briefly
Just a moment
Or two ago
Perhaps it's stuck
In this well-padded ceiling
Or maybe hidden some place
On this padded floor
Then again it just might be outside
This thick wooden doorknob-less door
Wherever it is
I lost it
I lost it
Some place
Some time ago

Milton Morrow
Milwaukee, WI

Power of Signing

Silence thundered across the table
Emotions carried through the hands
Faces reflecting the feelings expressed
Racing beyond time measured opinions

Focused on one amid those lost in many
Experiences filling voids left among strangers
Questions only shining into the blank stares of others
Fast and furious the exchanges of words

Felt much stronger than heard
Impacted upon the sight and mind
Experienced throughout one's being
Quiet is deafening when they depart

Verbal reflection pales in all their mirrors
Wondering how power rides these waves
Passed assured of understanding as sent
Remembered much more than screaming voices

Signing upon the winds of understanding
Powerful silence in very noisy confused world

William R. Spence
Shacklefords, VA

The past forty years have provided an interesting roller coaster ride of emotional highs and lows. Deployments, moving thirteen times, children, traveling and a career I loved made up my military period from 1977–98. Working as a Walmart crew member, Virginia employment interviewer, correctional officer, business owner, truck driver, and teacher have encompassed 1999–present. During this winding path of financial survival, there has been bankruptcy, family losses, renal cancer, kidney removal, open-heart valve replacement surgery, three bypasses, and eight grandchildren. The true poetic reality of why I am put together the book Warrior's Peace *in 2015 and continually keep submitting new poems to these anthologies, is the pinch of ego, teaspoon of uncertainty and the mountain of curiosity that these true expressions of my heart and soul might continue to capture a moment of someone's time.*

Symphony of Butterflies

Delicate white beauties
Like white tutu'd ballerinas
Plying their pliés,
Circling 'round the bushes
Dipping, sipping nectar,
Little trumpet blossoms
Heralding the sweetness.
Finding untapped reservoirs,
Drifting to another place,
Another bush and then…
Sweet melody is ended.

Jane P. KenKnight
Cincinnati, OH

"Symphony of Butterflies" was written in Tanzania when over one hundred butterflies of the same species landed on red and yellow trumpet blossoms until that group had thoroughly exhausted the nectar supply.

Fakeness

Everyone is after herself,
No one cares about you,
She faked her friendship
To use me, dominate me and take over my energy.

She's full of anger,
She wants to kill me.
Once she said,
"If I wanted to, I could crush her,"
About another one.

It wasn't meant for me at the time.
But now it is.

What a so-called friend.
She fooled me and now I realize it.

Daphne Martinez
San Juan, PR

Shameless

Shameless
Shameless
Of the life
I live for you

Shameless
Shameless
Of the faith
I committed to

In the eyes of many
I feel no shame
Of a faithful journey
I have in you

The way of the Lord
No one knows
Truth of the spirit
Encourages me on

Betty R. Patterson
Goshen, IN

To Us, All!

We know them as we see them now
A sparkling cheer of pink bouquets
As silent shadows sit upon the bough.

Growing wisdom and change intertwine
Creating a rarity of form
Maturing into a blend of fine wine.

Smiling eyes hide behind a glass of forgotten tears
A toast held high and given to the silent skies
As we drink down
  The tangled overflow
    Of years.

Nicolette R. Arrigo
Quakertown, PA

I learned to always try my best and fight the good fight, being a daughter of a World War II 82nd Airborne paratrooper and a strong-minded, hard-working English lady. My father's love of music and my mother's gift of writing magically gave me the inspiration to unite both through poetry. I became a teacher of English and music, leaving the profession after twelve years to be trained as a caregiver for my parents when tragedy struck. They still greeted each day with a smile and continued to fight the good fight. Their bond strengthened my beliefs.

92 Times Around

My 92 years have come and gone,
I am still blessed, healthy and strong.
I've had a very strange but good life,
Always trying to be a good mother and wife.
I was raised by Christians, Mom and Dad.
They loved us and gave us all they had.
All my children are sweet, loving and kind;
They bless me so much it blows my mind.
My phone rings — Can I bring you food?
Yes, if the weather's bad and you're in the mood.
They pick me up, take me out,
It's so nice — I love to be with them and ride about.
Bill got me a new car,
Much better than my old one by far.
A birthday gift — what a surprise — so beautiful,
It almost blinded my eyes.
When I can't add, subtract or check my mail,
A special one comes, gives my bail.
I try to be a blessing to all I meet,
So help me Jesus to always be sweet.
Thank you dear God for all my family and friends,
I am loved and blessed by all of them.

Thank you dear Jesus for loving me.

Lucille Tyler
Liberty, TX

Untitled

Miss our connection;
Know you must shift your focus.
Emily for life.

You are on your way
To the life of your choosing.
No stopping you now.

Hurts to stay away;
Connection at a distance.
Live, grow and expand.

I watch your life change;
Happy to be on the side.
Pride is without words.

Your wife to be shines…
Radiance of inner light
Sparkles in her eyes.

You sleep in her bed
Watching her soft and slow breaths.
She smiles… "I love you."

Michael Rausin
Upland, CA

Mother Earth, Father Sky

Mother Earth,
Father Sky, keep on
giving. Don't you
dry, your tearful
seas and food
supplies. Give us
hope. Make us
think, what we
may lose, if
we continue to
abuse, that
which we have,
sworn to protect.

Curtis L. Williams
Minneapolis, MN

Mercy

I was one of many flowers
Stretching when the sun rose,
Falling to sleep when the sun set,
Drinking from tears that fall from the sky.

I stand underneath stars and moon glow,
Watching helplessly while my companions die.

Until like so many others
 I too…
Felt the biting sob of death,
Dew trickled and I would cry.

Knowing every winter I'd disappear,
and then sun warmed the painted sky—
I'd come back!
Regaining renewed strength…
Though a flower does not know why.

Petals would fall and I'd metamorphosis,
Expanding my petals
With this,
Mercy…

Catherine J. Blystone
Waynesburg, PA

American Poet

Chicken Noodle Soup

This is about Wyatt who's ready
   to turn five; he loves to stop
   at puddles when we go out for
   a ride.
The sweet little guy has a really
   sweet soul, he invites me
   along wherever he goes.
When we go four-wheelin' he likes
   to ride with me, until my
   four-wheeler stops.
   Then he's ready to flee.
I take care of him about once
   a week, and one day he wanted
   to lick my feet.
When he comes to Mimi and Uncles
   he might want me to jump
   through a hoop, and fix him
   his favorite, a can of
   chicken noodle soup.

Mi Mi Sandy A. Kint
Orrtanna, PA

Don't Quit

When things go wrong as they
Sometimes will,
When the road you're on seems
All uphill,
When the funds are low
And your bills are high,
When you want to smile,
But you have to cry
When things are pulling
You down, rest, but don't
Quit
Life is queer with its
Twists and turns as every one
Of us knows.
Don't give up though the
Pace seems slow
You just may succeed
With another blow
You never can tell how close
You are, it may be near, when
It seems so far
So stick to the fight when you're
Hardest hit it's when things seem worst
That you must not quit

Evelyn Caputo
Somerville, NJ

Following the Call in His Footsteps

I wonder if people realize
How our boys leave home and risk their lives
To help keep freedom intact
Years on foreign battlefields are racked
Men have fought many battles
Because they knew what really matters
They go to war, many families left in tatters
Many worry everyday—can't be because of high pay
They go because they think it's the way
Have to have their priorities straight
Fight the battle for our fate
Joseph went, to Iraq, saw many things he can't erase, had to go
   back and trace
What happened to one's soldier who didn't come through
Hardest thing he had to do
To tell the mother at celebration's end
What had happened to his friend
Others had happy tears of gladness
After all the worry and sadness
But dampened by the loss of one
The mother who had lost her son
Now Patrick at a Marine base
So now begins again, the lonely wait and everyday fears to begin
Remind him he is in a long family line
From Civil War to present time

Elizabeth Thompson
Blandburg, PA

My ancestor joined the service at Cape Elizabeth, Maine, during the Civil War and another during the Spanish American War (served in the Philippines). Other family members have answered the call, in most others right up to the present time, including a cousin, a nurse, in WWII. She met and married a pilot in the Royal Air Force.

The Greatest Artist

When you awaken in the morning
and see the rising sun
you will be amazed at all the colors
and the day has just begun.

As you go outside
you look up at the sky.
You stand and stare
at the blue clouds floating by.

There are many flowers blooming
in colors bright and gay.
All these beautiful sights
change day by day.

Many pictures have been painted
by artists everywhere
but there is one artist
who paints with the greatest care.

If you take the time
to look at the rest
I am sure you will see
Jehovah God paints the best.

Mary Alice Seiter
Lexington, MI

The Beautiful Countryside

The buck and doe run side by side
Quickly as they run through the countryside

The wild red rose bushes are growing on the hillside there
As a light soft breeze fills the air

The dandelions are everywhere
As they pop up their yellow heads
To feel the spring breeze there
The squirrels are running up and down the trees having
Fun on this beautiful day
The robins are singing their songs as music fills the air
On this beautiful spring day
The world comes alive when spring is in the air
On the little countryside there

Bobbi Jo Hager
Ozark, AL

Stock of Self

I'm eighty-two years old,
I thank God daily for all His
Blessings of life
Love, liberty, freedom of religion
Health and happiness

My income is low monthly
Barely enough
Yet I do not go without
A family who cares
A pet to enjoy
Friends to call

For what more could I ask?

Gladys R. Witt
Hamersville, OH

Paris

The tower still stands, people
Fight back; lights shine through
The fog like cloud
Shining of Paris true color

Paris

Love all around from all over
People come together, getting
Ready for the holidays; smile,
But don't forget those who have lost

Paris

Lights shine bright, a prayer for
Hope for everyone and everything
The tower still stands
People fight back

Paris

The tower still stands!

Dianne Hill
Morris, IL

My dream is finally here—almost. My husband and son are so proud. Poems help me speak my mind when I am feeling sad. There is too much death, too many good cops, bad cops being played. Not enough love or belief in God. Holidays are for family, not to be spent at the graveyard.

Pigeons Come and Go

Gladys who was wheelchair bound, still managed to get around,
Going places wheelchair accessible, venturing out when able.
At home one day she heard a sound, and at the window she found,
There was a lone pigeon, one of the many among the city's legions.
On a whim she offered it some crumbs, unaware of the outcome;
Before long, it brought its friends, and many more without end.
Her home lease stipulated the feeding of animals was regulated,
An edict which if ignored, was equivalent to breaking the law.
When management was thus informed, a letter was duly drawn,
Choosing to ignore this legal missive, it too was dismissive.
When a summons came in, she awoke to the dilemma she was in,
Where to go? What to do? The solution she readily knew,
Not feeding them the solution, she'd abide by that resolution.
With winter soon encroaching and now the ending of fall,
How were the birds to cope with these changes at all?
Well, thinking again, survivors they were in any realm.
With the coming of Jack Frost the windows were now closed,
Gone forever were the friends that she now had surely lost.
One morning she thought she heard the sounds of many birds,
And as she had yearned, her beloved pigeons had now returned.
They were on sills, and on A/Cs and all around, the cooing sound!
They had come to bid adieu, to the most caring person they knew.
Then off they flew in a fell-swoop and turning for a final look,
Saw Gladys flying with them, free as a bird, and part of the brood.

Hilda Hanze
Ossining, NY

We only write because we do! Not everything we write is that good, but it speaks to us: a special place, thought or story we hope to express and share. Always like a newborn! Sometimes they come so fast! Sometimes you have to work for every word. Now you have given us a place in print where we can share. It's where my story becomes your story. That's what songs and poems do: make you feel and remember.

American Poet

Awakening

My younger self dreaded age
But I could not stop time.
The years have passed and I am holding
A bouquet of wisdom
Gathered from many earthly gardens.
All the stages of my life are sacred,
Even this, especially this,
As I move along a bridge of my infirmity
Connecting the increasing narrowness
Of my physical being
To the vast eternity of my soul.
I finger the petals of my bouquet
All at once knowing the difference
Between treasures of the earth
And treasures of heaven.

Diane Crawford
Selden, NY

Politicians Are Divided

Few politicians remain in the middle today
Most are on the left or right far away
When you stay in the middle
At the meeting when there is a debate
And the time is running late
You will solve the riddle
By staying in the middle
Those already on the far left or right
Stay stubborn in their fight
They think they are always right
So they never reach the middle
To solve the riddle
Because their minds are too far away
To the left or to the right
For them no words can come to light
So when the politicians disagree
We the American people cease to be free

Therese Jacques Gamache
Chepachet, RI

When I received the publisher's letter, I said to myself, I never wrote a poem about politicians before. I was afraid to fail, but the Lord provided. I always thank Him for a new poem or prose. I am having my fourth book of poems published by Eber & Wein. I give them away to friends. I was told, "You make people happy." It is charity to cheer someone up.

The Elegance of Union Station

The elegance of Union Station in the District of Columbia is unique if I remember correctly. I will never forget the adorning columns, walls and ceilings of the station. The elegance of Union Station in the District of Columbia represents the power, the boldness, and the prowess of the American government for the American people. The columns of Union Station were tall if I remember correctly. The columns inscribed the story of the American people from the time they were the original thirteen colonies, to the American Revolution, to the installment of General George Washington as the first president of the United States. The elegance of Union Station in the District of Columbia will never be forgotten. It tells the story of how a nation sprang into existence to support the people. The ceilings of Union Station were high; the lights of the station were hung from a height that if you looked up, you would be in awe.

The elegance of Union Station made you feel like you were someone when you entered or exited the premises. You received the presence of past presidents of the United States, and the past presence of famous people who walked on the grounds of Union Station. The elegance of Union Station will always be etched in my memory: the elegance of Union Station in the District of Columbia will always remind me that I received my degree from a university that was and still is located in a district where the main power of government is located: Washington, DC—the nation's capital, the main power of government which is the federal government.

Anthony Taylor
Brooklyn, NY

Guardian Angel

My guardian angel
Watching from above
With all your love
Shining down on us
We stay entranced
In a dream
Life is never as it seems
You left us here with broken hearts
Now you play a different part,
Instead of
Father,
Son,
Brother,
Cousin,
Uncle,
Or Grandmother
You are in Heaven
Our God has called you home
My guardian angel
We love you so
You'll always have a special
Place in our hearts,
As long as we remember
You'll never be forgotten
My guardian angel

Jessica Vollaro
Barrington, RI

This poem is dedicated to my grandmother, who passed away in July of 2006, and my cousin who passed away on February tenth of 2016, at the young age of thirty-nine. He leaves behind a two-and-a-half-year-old son, a fiancée and a family that is devastated by his passing as it was totally unexpected. May they rest in peace!

Wake-Up Calls

My wake-up calls started early in *1948*
When a near fatal car wreck was my fate
Recovery was slow, yet, life moves on
An early marriage in *1950*, a baby girl in '*53*,
When my husband found a girlfriend to replace *me*
My life stopped in every way, yet, the path I took
I wouldn't suggest; the road to Hell is not the best
From '*56* to '*72*, drinking, drugs; a second marriage
Then came a baby carriage: a beautiful baby boy
I had a good profession early on, my life was on a roll
I got sober in '*73*, and married one more time in '*75*
Another point in life, when I felt truly alive
In '*80* problems again, marriage #*3* coming to an end
I married again in '*86*
Life was good to *2002*
My husband passed away, my mother too
The pain of loss, surfaced one more time,
Today I'm up to age *83*
Grateful just to be, with many blessings along the way
Knowing all the choices I've made, got me up to today

Jó Ann Boggs Cordova
Hesperia, CA

Lessons learned along the way have truly got me up to today. Living with the "one day at a time" philosophy has been my saving grace through marriages, children, career, separations, divorce, and deaths of loved ones, including my twelve-year-old Yorkie, "Tillie B" (1932–present), is a true gift, in all that really matters in life (for me). Bottom line (for me): it is what it is… Peace of mind doesn't come easy. Enjoy life, "this is not a dress rehearsal."

Andrea Ireland Parker

I feel as though I shall write something devastating,
unto the literary world or just my world.
I often wonder which would have that,
greater effect upon my ego and state of being.
Greatness is all about me shown through,
A constant dance of infallible little charms,
Which dangle about my solid grasp,
Will I ever be what I feel?

For days I have wanted to write something,
in the name of Andrea Ireland Parker.
In the beginning it all seemed so perfectly
innocent a thing to want to do. I then set forth with perfectly,
high ambition of getting across my feelings and deepest thoughts.
I might have just assumed to scale Mount Everest.

An endless journey it always seems, chasing a dream,
that can never ever be. I cannot release all the love I have inside.
There is no answer… no solution to my angst felt deep.
How is it possible to feel so left out ever stung by chills of isolation,
is there no fine way out for me?

Steve Arlington King
Brooklyn, NY

This is dedicated to Andrea Ireland Parker of the University of New Mexico class of 1978, unquestionably my very best friend from 1973 through 1978. Although she was well aware of my poetic endeavors, I never displayed this, particular, poem to her. Eventually we lost touch with one another, and I have often prayed that she has enjoyed a very good life.

My Folk's Genealogy

My great-great-grandfather—whom
I never knew… was related to President
Woodrow Wilson—it's true! My other
great-grandparents in genealogy were
connected to Pocahontas, and Daniel
Boone. There's other famous people—
just too many names for me to refer to!
In past years as a mother of teenagers—
I'd lived in Virginia on the Pocahontas
Trail. That's where George Washington
visited and dwelt. Well, Truman was
President when I was born. Those were
hard times when some folks felt forlorn!
Back then a dime was like a dollar. I'm
not rich or famous—as it might be nice
to be. And in past years I was invited
to Washington, DC—even though
a simple way of life must have been
meant for me. I didn't get to go.
But my great-uncle met JFK,
and his brother Robert too; I was a
teenager then! I've traveled this country
far and wide, plus been overseas as
an Army wife!

Frances Elaine Camp
Americus, GA

Reading Woodrow Wilson's poem in your letter inspired me to mention the presidents' names in my poem of "My Folk's Genealogy." I recall one true story of my mother's father as a teenager running with others alongside Roosevelt's car when he visited our hometown of Wellston, Ohio! In the sixties Nixon was on a train that stopped behind where my other grandfather had lived: to greet people! I'd seen Eisenhower's house in the early seventies. My Army husband met Ford, Nixon, Reagan, and Carter. I met Jimmy and RosaLynn Carter in past years.

The Gift

How to start, think of ideas that are dropping in.
Some float by, others shout to begin.
Clear your mind and let the words flow free.
Welcome the gift and enjoy the story.
Don't worry about perfection, this can block the flow.
Just get the idea down, before you let it go.
Tidying up and finding words can be done, but later
Once you get the idea down, you have claimed your gift.
Let yourself be like a twig in the river floating in the drift.
The more you leave your mind and heart open to receive,
The less you will have to do after to retrieve.
Get down words that have been given, cherish and share
Around the words that have come to you, like writing on a cloud.
They come inside your brain, or you can speak out loud.
People are ideas people, or they are not,
But we can all learn to be better, trying every day.
I'm grateful always that my imagination has full say.
Accept the gift, but use with care,
To enrich life's long love affair.

Ann Gallant
Marshall, TX

So, We're Over 65

Have you awakened to learn you are over 65?
Well, I have and not surprised I just smiled.
How days go by and we don't dare to notice,
Our fixed ways, our wrinkled arms and face.

Then we say to ourselves, so we're over 65,
We still have lots of miles and a lot of drive.
If you think about it, it is a privilege,
It is a blessing to be breathing at this age.

So let us celebrate, let us be thankful to be here,
We are on Earth but once, help the world be better.
While we can, let us be mentors, be a good example,
Savor life, be beautiful, be positive and joyful.

At the same time, be cautious and be careful,
The world is uncertain, don't be afraid, just enjoy.
If you go on a date, don't pick up the check,
Guard your social security, it's there until death.

Life is what we signed up for and before we know,
We will be called home, no exception… me and you.
Then we realize that the best is yet to come,
With our last smile and our work on Earth is done.

So, we're over 65! It's not that bad.

Virgilia A. Smith
Marshall, MI

Ah… getting older! Time goes so fast. It's just like we blink an eye and realize we're over sixty-five! Written on August 19, 2015, this is from the heart and dedicated to everyone over sixty-five. This is also a song with a pending copyright. I am now a seventy-year-old RN… still working in the emergency department at a local hospital. I thank the Lord for all the blessings He has given me and my family. Truly, "every day is a gift from God, and every moment of that day is in His hands." Praise the Lord… I trust in You.

End to Everything

There is an end to everything.
The sun parts from the sky in the evening.
There is an end to love.
Leaves fall off the branches in the fall.
The best of friends must part.
*Everything in this world is temporary—even the world itself
is temporary.
Let's not shed tears because I believe that the world is round,
and the place which may seem like the end may also be only the
beginning when each season chases after the next one while each
month ends its mission as December passes its baton to January
every single year!

*2 Corinthians 4:18

Andrew K. Ha
Gibbstown, NJ

Poetry creates a unique world in which words are exquisitely condensed into a unified whole peculiar to the poet. This poem has been born of what is described about the world in the New Testament—2 Corinthians 4:18—that perspicuously depicts the nature of the planet. Despite such a transient duration characterized by humanity, the poet is hopeful about the bright side of human existence.

America the Great

What is happening to this great nation of ours?
Do we not know we could be in our last hours?

Our leaders must heed the warnings before it's too late,
Or I shudder to think of what could be our fate.

God must be brought back into our nation,
Before He in His infinite mercy loses His patience.

Make time to hold the Lord ever so near.
With Him in your heart there is nothing to fear.

He wants us to be brave and bold,
Our faith and trust in our lives hold.

Be ready every day from the Lord do not part,
Be sure you stay strong and keep the Lord in your heart.

God bless America.

Marshelle Carberry
Fresno, CA

Outlook

Astrology will always stay to
plan our lives day by day…

There are so many signs so strong,
which come to light as we go along…

God gives us certain people we look to,
who work the star system for me and you…

Our future is planned, our loves are too,
as we gaze into the midnight blue…

If you're looking for the real answer,
seek out the person with the sign of Cancer…

There is Capricorn, Taurus, and Aries too,
which are just a few to see you through…

So, as you know, sooner or later the stars
all point to "our creator"…

Oleta P. Braley
Rochester, NY

American Poet

By the Grace of God

Against all odds, we are now a nation, who once was a servant
   where freedom was just a dream.
Thoughts such as this were left unspoken, but, not allowed
   to flourish.
The American spirit could not be diminished when faced
   with adversity.
Many good men and women have fallen and will fall to seek justice
   for one and all.
We, the people, must find the courage to forge ahead and seek the
   truth, to wake from the darkness of oppression,
To search for the guiding light of what is right and true for the red,
   white and blue.

Marie E. Belensky
Taylor, PA

I have always wanted to be a writer to express my thoughts and feelings on paper. Living in a free nation as an American citizen I have that privilege. God bless America and all it stands for. To all of the men and women who have fought to keep this nation safe, I thank you and I salute your courage. I'm in your debt always.

A Wonderful Night

You called me a romantic
Yes, I guess you're right:
I thought it just fantastic
The way you spoke to me that night.

A chance to view paradise
Like I never dreamed I'd see,
But then I'm just not wise
To the way things seem to be.

The evening was simply divine,
A full moon in the sky;
Heaven was surely mine
Need I ask, but why?

To be blessed with your touch
Feel your warm sweet kiss:
The pleasures were much
In a glorious night of bliss:

Just like Cinderella
Prince Charming came my way,
Such a gallant fella
To steal my heart away!

Then here it is, tomorrow
The time when all dreams end,
But there will not be sorrow;
Hopefully I made a new friend!

So in the memories of my life
This beautiful evening I'll store!

Daisyann B. Fredericks
Canajoharie, NY

The Brave Soldiers

The brave soldiers fight for our country, so we could have freedom. The brave soldiers are like stars, because they all shine so bright. The brave soldiers are full of devotion and love for America. Soldiers deserve their recognition and respect. They sacrifice so much and also put their lives on the line, when they leave their families at home behind. Soldiers risk their lives in wars. They are truly amazing heroes. That's why I have so much love and respect for them. Also the uniform they have on, it represents a purpose. That purpose is the bravery and being selfless. Let's continue to salute and honor all the brave soldiers, all the men and women who ever served, all past, present and future brave soldiers.

Malik Gayden
Rochester, NY

I wrote this poem from my heart for all the soldiers for their sacrifices and dedication. I am more authentic in my poetry. I have written so many extraordinary poems, so much more that my next step is to put out my own poetry book. I have written over sixty new poems that display my full artistic vision. I hope this poem makes an impact. I wrote this poem with tears in my eyes. Thank you, Eber & Wein Publishing, for always recognizing my true talent in poetry. Being a part of this iconic book with other talented poets is an honor.

Vol. 1

I Miss Love

Love is not outgrowing love and not
trading love for what the world has to offer.
Holding on to love in times of woe, and in
the times of happiness, the real true love
that is not found in the hearts of
material possessions. A tender walk through
the woods with your brother before he
goes off to Vietnam, what could be traded
for that, the smile of your little sister
When she hands you a Coke, when Coke
was still a nickel. Love is like taking
these pictures with your eyes, and storing
them in your heart and mind, where they will
never get lost. Love is in your heart
whether you live in a mansion on a hill
or a little shack out in the woods. Love
is holding on and hanging in. True love
does not smother and make demands,
love is understanding. Capturing love is in
your heart like a child, before the harsh
realities of life sat in. God is love.
God please bring back love that's all that
will restore this nation and world.
I miss love.

Marilyn Love
East Bernstadt, KY

When Duty Calls

Let us stand tall
When duty calls
Let us keep our fathers, mothers,
Aunts, uncles, sisters and brothers.
Here on American land,
Let us hold our own hands.
Let other countries fight their own wars,
Don't let the American's death soar.
We have lost enough women and men,
Our hearts will never mend.
Some by death some by PTSD,
Because we sent them overseas.
Let us stand tall,
When duty calls.
Keep them here on American land,
Thank them and shake their hand.

Virginia Gail Lassiter
Plant City, FL

Beastly Beauty

Galloping through the tall grass,
I emerged into a knight of
heavy armor.

Ambushed by her scalloped nails,
she dug through the steel
of my chest,
clawing deeply, wounding every scour
of belief I had ever known.

She seemed so glorious,
defiant, and from the finest quality of beauty,
but underneath
her calloused eyes was a dark array
of destruction,
a powerful stroke of filthy inheritance.

She drug her heels
down the gravel path into the night.

I sat scorned and motionless
as blood poured from the wounds
I bestowed by such a beast —
gasping one last breath,
defeated.

She seemed as any other being,
but at night,
she turned into a wrath
of undefined mythical creature.
Never underestimate the aura of one's soul....

Beck Tripp
Great Bend, KS

Gifts

The memory is full
Your understanding and giving
Your measured praise or
  gentle reminder
Guidance along the narrowing path
Countless events while sharing
  the climb
Always accompanied, watched
  over with care
Store all away, gifts of the heart
From the now mature younger
For the weakening elder
Remember, recall with detail
Each gift of the heart

Lois M. Aiken
Arlington, MA

Amazing Love

God's amazing love for you and me
He sent his Son to set us free
Amazing love how could it be
He laid down his life for you and me
He arose again and lives today
In his celestial home far away
His Cross is our bridge that spans the great divide
That separates life on Earth from our eternal side
Amazing love for you and me
Through God's love we are set free
When our life on earth is done
We can live with God's eternal Son
Through God's love we have been redeemed
Jesus Christ the Savior of us all

John Brannick
Colby, KS

A Summer Visit with My Brother Jim's Family

I sit and relax,
After long hard day at work,
And chat with my brother Jim,
On hot humid evening,
And with his wife Gloria,
And their three kids Jim, Jennifer, Jake,
Bon Jovi rocks on their radio,
As we spend good quality time together,
Eating pizza, cheeseburgers—drinking Pepsi Cola,
In living room of their country home north of Granville,
While their dogs Cochise and Reba sit nearby,
Talking work, school, weather, fishing, sports,
We're having fun as it's nearly dusk,
Cut grass fragrance through windows,
I'm glad I'm spending the night,
We'll watch *Star Trek* on TV,
Sharing garden vegetables,
As their cool fans hum

William D. Irwin
Princeton, IL

This is dedicated to my brother Jim who had a great life, had a wonderful family with a wife and kids who loved him very much, made a lot of great friends, and had a lot of great times. We all loved him very much and we all have very fond memories of doing many cherished things together all during our lives. Yes... Jim was a hero—doing what he wanted to do, being what he wanted to be, and always doing and being his very best.

A Puppy in the Alley

There was a puppy in the alley
when I pulled in today
and just as soon as he saw me
started to walk away.

He stopped and took another look
with tears in his eyes
and looked like he's been crying —
caught me by surprise.

And he just stood there shaking,
I knew he was cold.
I could tell that he was a puppy
and wasn't very old.

Now he was not wearing a collar,
maybe had no home.
Someone probably put him out;
now he has to roam.

That was when I'd asked myself,
should I take him in?
I wondered if he had his shots
and where he's been.

When I see pets on the streets
in this kind of weather
I get a feeling they've got no home;
I'd like to get together.

I would take them and feed them
like I've done before
with the kittens and squirrels
out by my front door.

Cleatus Cherokee Lee Murdaugh
Chicago, IL

American Poet

Tribute to Our Flag

If there will be only one flag of our nation
flying high in the sky
respect her wherever they take her—
our forefathers fought for her
on many battlefields of the world
dirty from mud, but never fall

How proud we are of our flag
that flies high in the sky on the moon
and under the sea—
and many places of the world
for the victory and the freedom,
for those who pray for help

And they bring her home from the war
and march with her on the street
of our cities and towns—
and people cheered her up with applause
no matter how she looks,
we respect with pride and dignity

Otto Valnoha
Fox Lake, IL

The Old Folks

We are told we are the old folks
That live down the road a ways
They say we are the lucky ones
As we lived back in the good old days

But for us it's rather lonely:
So many have now passed on
We can no longer go see old friends
As they are now in the great beyond

No more can we call old neighbors
With a crank of the telephone?
As the only numbers they have now
Are engraved on their tombstone

Many good friends are gone forever
Never again will we hear them say
Come by our house tomorrow night
And help us pass the time away

So let us not forget the memory
Of old friends of the good old days
For we are now called the old folks
That live down the road a ways

Leeland Wilson
Evart, MI

The older we get the more we realize that our age group is a lonely time in life, as so many have passed on. How great it was to step to the box on the wall and give a few cranks of the handle and talk to several neighbors at a time. So they might be right in saying we are the lucky ones for having lived in the good old days.

Ruining the World

Thanks Osama Obama,
For ruining my world.
The stock market drops —
There are no jobs,
Everybody cries and sobs.
People think it's time to rob.
Gas is high — roads are full —
The gates at the border
Are wide open —
"If you are a Muslim
Terrorist — welcome home!"
"I want to be king!"
Cries Obama — "now!"
Go back to Kenya —
They will welcome you
With open arms.
Go somewhere else,
Where you will cause
No more harm.
Take Hillary and
Bill with you please!
To a place far away,
So America can be free.
And the flag can wave in peace.

Marc B. Stein
San Diego, CA

The Journey's End

It has been a long road
To the journey's end.
Some never make it.
Others still descend.

The road ahead is rocky
Full of rocks and thorns.
Each day is a new day
It's time to try once more.

Each day is a new one
No two are the same.
Yet on down the road
It's a struggle all the way.

Don't give up the journey
Wait for what tomorrow brings.
It could be entirely different
In so many ways.

Don't let Satan tempt you
It's not the will of God.
His direction leads you
To a place that you don't want.

Jo Biraben
La Habra, CA

The Light in Me

I am me in my own way.
I am who I am in a very unique way.
Weak and strong, living and dying, and reborn again.
Happy and sad with a determination to carry on, not only in good
  times but bad times as well.
But as I live and walk on this earth, I carry with me a light, which
  I use to help in life no matter who I come in contact with.
Showing love, understanding, friendship for the caring of
  many people.
I am who I am for Jesus is in me, for He is the light of the world.
For His light of faith is in me to carry. For the light is in me.

Debbie J. McGinnis
Bedford, OH

"The Light in Me" was written on January 2, 1980. This was when I began writing poems, as I took a creative writing class while I was a student at Bedford High School. This poem is dedicated to my uncle, Daniel J. Krujch, who went home to be with Jesus on Tuesday January 19, 2016. "I love you, Uncle Dan, and I will see you again," your niece Debbie.

Miss Liberty

Standing proudly in New York Harbor
Proclaiming that our land is free
She is the symbol of our freedom,
America's pride — Miss Liberty

Cast in France — shipped to the US
Back in eighteen hundred eighty-four
As a token of the friendship
Of our two countries forevermore

A symbol to the multitudes
Eagerly arriving on our shore,
Each praying that a better life
Is waiting inside the US door

The largest statue ever made
Her copper gleaming in the night
A symbol of liberty and freedom
Standing for the just and right

Perched high upon her pedestal,
Her torch three hundred feet above
She radiates the American dream
Of worldwide freedom, peace and love

Billie L. Wolfe
Bryan, OH

Trump's Triumph

Billionaire Trump appears well on his way
    to become the next President, USA
Sometimes, regrettably, haughty and crude,
    he is in sync with a general mood.
He touches a nerve of common concern
    for a Latino presence wherever you turn.
Judging Congress inept, to the nth degree,
    rings true to millions who do agree.
Trump's election will perhaps be assured
    if military/industrials get his word:
"We will rearm!" in a Trump declaration,
    cheering MIs across the nation.
They pledge their support as they do rely
    on high rewards for military supply.
It worked for Hitler eight decades ago
    and it may work as well for Trump also.
"Beware of military/industrial ties!"
    was Ike's warning, so very wise.
His warning ignored the past fifty five years,
    brought $trillions in debt,
        oceans of blood,
            rivers of tears.

Philip N. Martin
Tulsa, OK

Caring Angel

An angel came into my house.
I was in a very bad way,
Caring for my elderly spouse —
Twenty-four hours everyday.

My kids knew I needed help —
Called an agency to get care.
The angel came, my heart did melt
She is an answer to my prayer.

Caregivers are special indeed.
To them more than a job to do
Taking care of a client's needs
Giving respect that they need, too.

My angel comes everyday twice.
She's cheerful, making the time go.
Many of the tasks are not nice.
There is no complaining I know.

I will not send my spouse away.
Never a thought in my head,
Having my spouse home everyday
Is manageable instead.

So grateful she came into my life,
My depression's begun to lift.
I'm still my husband's loving wife
And having him home is a gift.

Sandra Kisler
Othello, WA

I dedicate my poem, "Caring Angel," to my husband's caregiver, Laura Ayala, and her family: husband Lupe and children Alex, Mireya and Nayeli. Caring for my husband of fifty-four-plus years is something I now can do with their help. Writing poetry has given me a way to lessen stress, giving me something else to think about. I started writing poems years ago as a hobby, and now it's a need.

Lonely

Our house is very empty
Because you are not here
My life is very lonely
It's more than I can bear

I think about you often, morning noon and night
I dream about you kissing me and holding me so tight

We loved each other for sixty-three years
When I talk about you
My eyes fill up with tears

I will always feel you near
Even though we are apart
Happy memories and my love for you
Will forever fill my heart

Beverly Ogman
Boynton Beach, FL

The Valley

One day I climbed a mountain, and when I
reached the top I stopped and looked down.
There was the most beautiful scene:
a valley.
In the middle of the valley was a pond.
Little off from the pond was a small hill cover
in purple flowers. I looked back at the pond,
and from the hill came two beautiful white
swans, they went into the pond and they began to
swim together enjoying the peace.
That peace wasn't going to last long.
For rain clouds came overhead, bringing rain, the
rain didn't last long, it moved away leaving a
beautiful rainbow and bring back that peace, and
the swans continued to swim in that pond in the
midst of that valley below. What a beautiful
valley of peace, below a mountain.
There are many valleys around the world with
many different stories to tell:
a farm, a small village, a church, a snow scene, and
of course a pond.
Every valley has a different story, a story in every
country around the world.

Carol A. Miller
Washingtonville, NY

I can imagine what it would be like to climb Mt. Everest, the highest known mountain in the world: reaching its crest, and at the top, taking time out to look below, into the valley, and looking as far as the eyes can see, what many stories can be told, not only of the valley, but experience of climbing that mountain.

Chipmunks

Tina hadn't been in her basement for well over a month,
She said it was because of those crazy little chipmunks.
The last time she was in her basement, those crazy little guys
   jumped on her back and tried getting into her hair.
She ran through the basement stumbling on the steps, on her way
   upstairs. She slammed the door shut and tried to rejoice.
But those guys were climbing walls and slamming into floor joist.
Sandy said to get Jim: He'll put on the run,
Tina said, Yea he'll probably still have fun.
The next morning I said, Why not have a little fun,
As I gather up a knife and my double-barrel shotgun.
When I opened the basement door, what to my surprise,
There were, like, ten or twelve of those little guys,
They were jumping, snarling and growling at me.
I fired a couple shots, okay maybe three;
When I went down in the basement there were blood, guts and
   strips all over the walls.
Most of those guys were dead, but there was one trying to crawl,
I took my knife and tried to put an end to it all, but there was one
   trying to hang on as he slid down the wall.
Tina came down the steps the walls were pink and the windows
   were shattered,
Tina said, We got those guys and that's all that matters.
If you want to get rid of a varmint, and still have a little fun, give
   Jim a call.
He will bring over a knife and a double-barrel shotgun.

James B. Brown
Saxton, PA

Brothers in Arms

He stood in somber,
with his head bowed down.
As around his neck,
The Medal of Honor was placed.
    For gallantry beyond the call,
For the many lives that were saved.
But for the few who fell,
For them he gave praise.
    For they were his brothers in arms,
All were of the same squad.
But he was the lone survivor,
Of that night, on guard.
    And with his bullet-riddled body,
As the last shot was fired.
He stopped a platoon of soldiers,
From coming through the wire.
    With their bodies strewn,
All over the ground.
His machine gun was silenced,
As he to, went down.
    And after a time,
His wounds had healed.
But his heart still bleeds,
For his brothers, that were killed.
    And so this medal they hung,
Around his neck, this day.
He placed it on the monument,
Of his brothers, who had fallen, as if to say.
    Thank you my beloved brothers,
For if not for your courage and fight,
I too might have fallen,
And as for this medal,
I've earned not the right.

Lawrence Melvin
Greenup, KY

American Poet

San Francisco

Of all the cities in which I've been
The one well worth remembering
Is the one that's high above the bay
Where you can see the fog and sunshine play
From Grand Nob Hill and Coit Tower,
You can see Mt. Tamalpais flower
Wander Chinatown and High Twin Peaks
Visit Civic Center where the city speaks
From Golden Gate Park to Fleischaker Zoo
There's so much for you and me to do
Like crossing "The Bridges" late at night
It's really a tremendous sight!
The food and drink are beyond compare
From the "Top of the Mark" to Union Square
Tony Bennet was oh so right
This, like Paris, is a city of light
I love you Baghdad by the bay,
And sometime I'll come home to stay!

Norm Smith
Columbus, OH

Adam and Eve

Adam and Eve,
Alfred and Ethel,
Alfred enjoys
Ethel's bethel,
A and E—
Arts and Entertainment.

Alfred loves Ethel,
Ethel loves Alfred,
We're married,
We have carried
Our love along
For 37 years.

We will be married
For 37 more years,
But our love
Will last forever,
Through this poem,
And ever.

Alfred Elkins
Bronx, NY

Kisses and Roses

Walking through the garden of flowers
I had stopped to smell the roses
And it was there that I found her
She looked so pretty and mature
The air was misty and so fragrant
It was then I was kissed by a rose
That moment I realized life matters
To be kissed by a Rose of Maria
Life is like walking through a garden
We should all enjoy the beauty of life
Walking through the garden of life
It's like walking through the garden of flowers
And like flowers so are the people
Some you pick as friends that last
And so the flowers are enjoyed

Tyrone Glessner
Sacramento, CA

This poem is being dedicated to my wife Maria. She is such a beautiful and great woman. My wife has brought me such inspiration, joy and a greater perspective on life. Happy tenth anniversary to my sweetheart (January 12, 2016).

Abandoned House in Winter

How much can be left (of you)?
Handprint frozen
On cold winter window,
Dim, shadow of a face,
Behind aged, frosted, cracked glass,
Someone I used to know (years ago),
Standing on the porch now,
Anxiety filtering through my veins,
This old-two story, abandoned farm house,
Front door unhinged, with broken padlock,
Edge of light slices through and umbrellas across
The dirt and broken glass-covered floor,
Torn white veil gauze curtains shifting in the breeze.
How much can be left of you?
I saw you once there, through the window,
Your naked, frail, transparent ghost figure.
On this day of winter's first frozen snow,
This old house, abandoned for years,
Your slight handprint remains
Frozen inside the windowpane.
Your face remains,
An ice shadow drawn against the window.
Even though, it's been years and years ago,
I can still feel you, see you,
A ghost who lives behind the glass
Of my heart and mind.

G. L. Bass
Pleasant Prairie, WI

Blessings Everywhere

I can't believe each day;
I open my eyes and know
that I have been blessed in every way.
It doesn't matter large or small;
do you appreciate the universe overall
or look for a blessing in a great land fall?

From now on look to the sky;
feel the warmth of the new day sun
and feel the air when the rain is done.
Do we need more, in this life so grand,
than what God has given
without any other demand?

All the birds and flowers of the earth,
do not look for a way to attain the good;
they trust that life will unfold as it should.
The universe is a magnificent place
all we see can be good in this space.
Don't look too far it has been given with grace.

Dolores Kutzer
Erie, PA

Baker

God bless you Baker,
My friend of many years
I know you are just a dog
Your loss brings me to tears

You loved me unconditionally
Always by my side,
Now that we must depart
I must take this all in stride

You will not be forgotten
As my truck buddy of all time
Always laying just beside
No way my feelings be blind

God will give me another golden
Your pictures hang on my wall
Of a faithful servant, I dearly loved
When God had made His call

Yes you are only allowed
A certain time on earth
And when your number's called
You will meet your maker and rebirth

I will see you in the skies beyond the clouds

Darryl Ehlers
Lynden, WA

Below Low

My unwanted disease is again fully aware,
It's thrown my day's plans into the depths of the seas!
How long will I feel like I'm useless and unwanted?
How long to be knocked backwards, bloodying my knees?

I can't make myself smile, because you smile at me!
I can't make myself move, when you suggest ideas to me.
I don't even see you, so why bother you stay here?
My sanity's desperately trying to successfully mutiny!

When the fist of depression hits square on the throat,
I can't say loving words, I can't push or pull!
All these years and I still easily get knocked down.
My darkness is deeply growing; I'm now below low!

Below low,
I can walk under a pregnant ant, without bending down!
Below low,
Depression reigns complete, bastard's wearing his crown!

Jeff Culling
Hollywood, FL

Black Is Beautiful

We should always be proud of who we are!
God has blessed so many of us to become stars!
Walk with dignity, my friends. Let it show, like the cool winds.
Many blacks are very courageous and strong.
"Say It Loud, I'm Black and I'm Proud," is one of my favorite songs.
Our people have the most beautiful skin in the world.
There are many shades of color.
Use your talents to the fullest.
Each one of us has God-given talents.
We determine our own destiny.
Everybody was created with equality.
Blacks have made history in education, medicine, politics, television, music, sports, fashion, modeling, poetry, and as entrepreneurs/business owners.
Ebony and *Essence* magazines have made Black History.
African Americans have the victory!
The Essence Festival makes millions of dollars every year.
I will give it a whopping cheer!
It has been celebrated in New Orleans since 1994 to present.
The city is shaped like a crescent.
What a great event it is for blacks to attend!
The participants' gifts are what we commend!
Several blacks have become millionaires (Sean Combs aka Diddy, Robert Johnson, Tiger Woods, Earvin Johnson Jr., Shawn Carter aka Jay Z, William Henry Cosby, Sheila Johnson, and R. Donahue Peebles).
Three African Americans are billionaires (Aliko Dangote — the world's wealthiest Black person, Oprah Winfrey is the world's first female black billionaire, and Michael Jordan).
Remember, God made all of us.

Jacklin P. Brinston
Port Gibson, MS

I'm from Port Gibson, Mississippi, and I was born November 16, 1956. I have a BA in elementary education and worked as a teacher. My hobbies are reading and making arts and crafts. My greatest achievement is becoming a writer. I took a course in journalism when I was a junior in high school (1973). It was very interesting to me! But, I was very amazed when I began writing poems in November of 2012. Since then, I have been constantly writing poems. Keep in mind, I am an evacuee from Hurricane Katrina in New Orleans. I moved to Mississippi in September 2005. This is what inspired me to write the poem "Black Is Beautiful!"

Great Nation

Full of color and glory
united, undivided

Through hardship, harsh war within,
attacks and troubles without,

Hear the history cadence
trembling turbulences,

Hear the echoing begin
ghostlike marching, tramping boots,

Left, right, left right, forward march
lefts, rights, lefts, rights, forward march,

One nation, ours, one nation
under God, under our God

Linda M. Freemyer
Maryville, MO

Quiescent Child

The arm is moving up and down
A bell is ringing, no, clanging
Standing tall a form in a habit
I move a thousand ways, foreboding

A language so foreign hits my ears
My eyes are darting back and forth
Grasping at words making no sense
My ears listening not one, but both

Sitting down quietly at my desk
To seize a language, I don't understand
To get a grip with my head cast down
I am a stranger in my homeland

A ruler lands on a desk
Ringless finger attached to it
The habit turns and walks away
Relief settles, I am not the culprit

Boots laced up to her knees
Gnarled hand swinging at the side
Must have died at ninety
Born again at ninety, a riptide

My head fills of home
Drunk with dreams of safety
Home, take me back home
Where my ancient tongue is a festivity

Florence Richmond
Wauconda, IL

Story of Job

Hear the story of Job, God-fearing man of old
Amassed wealth, family, silver and gold.
Lost all for the devil, then doubting friends
Said Job's troubles were God's punishment for sins.

For their remarks Job took exception to
Saying their statements were not true.
Recalling his life, loving God, being humble and kind,
Striving to be just ever on his mind.

Job prayed humbly, begging God to explain
Reasons for his trials, sorrows and pain.
The almighty spoke freely and without doubt,
Explained what Heaven, nature and living was about.

Job, through misery, sorrows and tribulations,
Begged God to bless his friends, revelations
Portrayed all his troubles blessings in disguise.
God's word forever upholds Job great and wise!

Hulda K. Sellingsloh
Hopewell Junction, NY

I was born November 29, 1912, in South Texas to cotton farmers Henry and Hulda Knipling; I was the last of twelve children. My purpose in life is to be a force for good. I first became an attorney, then married and had four children. At age fifty, I began to study artistic painting — with success. I then became a promising poet with three honors. My poem "Story of Job" will hopefully benefit a troubled world, recalling the time of Job, thus promoting prayers for harmony among friends and all nations.

The Last Toast (of the Doolittle Raiders)

The men were as old as the vintage cognac
The seal finally broken, a toast their last act
Out of the eighty, only four remain
The rest of these heroes are freed from their pain

Alongside the brandy, each man had his cup
When his time was over his cup was turned up
They came once a year to make roll-call and toast
Remembering with reverence and nary a boast

Into Japan, the Raiders flew
Led by General Doolittle who
Bombed the enemy
(Those who slew our allies, and those at Pearl Harbor, too)

Some were captured, some were dead
The survivors pondered their fate with dread
They called it "the war to end all wars"
Some gave their life, all carry the scars

They helped turn the tide with American pride
So here's to the Raiders and their midnight ride!

Janet Sue Deckard
Texas City, TX

Mockingbird and Me

Mockingbird is perched up in the tree
   Thinking he is hiding there from me
But rustling leaves are giving him away,
   Well—now I must move on, I cannot stay

Suddenly he flies up to the sky
   Singing—is he mocking me good-bye?
With happiness abounding since he's free
   To fly away, not grounded here like me

The lovely, happy music he provides
   Cheers me while I ponder now what lies
Ahead of me this day—but it won't be
   With the happiness of flying free

Or maybe he is calling out to me
   Singing, I know that you are not my enemy
If only you had wings so you could fly
   Together we'd sail up to Heaven in an azure sky

We entertain the thought but know instinctively
   God created us to serve Him faithfully
For birds to sing their songs of joy so cheerfully
   While we spread love, fulfill needs of humanity

Pat Evan
Austin, TX

On a morning walk I experienced the contact with a mockingbird as written in the first three verses. The last two verses are a mix of my imagination and beliefs. I am a transplanted Texan and the mockingbird's trill has captured my heart. Our outdoor sounds are left to city traffic in winter when they leave to go even further south. But, happily, in early spring their joyful song fills the air once again.

I Ask the Lord to Bless You

I ask the Lord to bless you,
Each and every day.
I ask the Lord to bless you,
In everything you do and say.

I ask the Lord to bless you,
Keep you close to Him.
I ask the Lord to bless you
Again and again.

I ask the Lord to bless you
In your daily life.
I ask the Lord to bless you
Keep you in His sight.

I ask the Lord to bless you,
This prayer I will send.
I ask the Lord to bless you
Each day that you begin.

Althea Lani
Ely, NV

I am the mother of three children — two girls and a boy — a grandmother of nine grandchildren, great-grandmother of six, and married fifty-six years. I wrote this poem for a dear friend who was having some family difficulties at the time. I have written poems since the age of ten years old and am inspired by a word or action. I hope this poem will help others who may be having the same issues.

Freedom Scenes

This is indeed hallowed ground
As one can clearly see
Displaying nature's gifts and
Blessings of sweet liberty
Observe the labor of a farmer
Planting crops he has faith will rise
The care, and confidence of a mother
Holding her child by her side
Teachers in their classroom chalk in hand
Instructing tomorrow's leaders of our land
Churches of different faiths on many corners
Ever praying for more peace and grace
Asking God to help them change their
Sometimes wicked ways
America, America, how truly blessed we are
For God has placed us in his loving hand
And brought us all from afar
Now through his range of people colors
Black, yellow, brown or white
All are encouraged to display his inner light
Thus this rainbow of colors now seen
Distributed throughout the land
Make it clear our country reflects
A picture of God's perfect plan
Thus red, white and blue God truly loves you

Jasper McGee
Vacaville, CA

Where Have All the Statesmen Gone?

Only a few still understand freedom
and leave of their own volition:
knowing power is in the people
to unseat them at each election.
The more prolonged their stay
the more corruption beckons.
Where are the Washingtons of today
to do the people's work,
with honesty and integrity,
denying each bribe or royalty?
To return to their homes
when their duty is done
and encourage liberty in our young.
To stand in the face of injustice
even when chances are slim,
fighting for right causes
against the cultural whim;
following the written laws:
the Constitution and founding papers,
understood at the time
by each citizen and layperson.
Decades of distraction
have waylaid the moral ground
in pursuit of personal gratification.

Rhonda C. Villanova
Ellington, CT

The Courageous

The courageous come in many forms
From local heroes to those who fight the desert storms
Many wear blue uniforms and patrol along the street
Some heavy gear for against the fire they must compete
Others may have outfits that allow them to blend in
But each of these brave souls all fight to win
Against the crime of everyday life
Against the troubles, accidents, and strife
Against those whose goal is to rule
Against the oppressors whose ways are cruel
They fight for the people to make their own choice
They fight so that everyone can have a voice
They fight to give all a living chance
They fight for freedom and independence

Kayla Evans
Wayne, MI

Where Have You Gone Art Garfunkel?

I wonder if Art Garfunkel
Continues to have a great voice.
So many years have gone by
Since he separated from Paul Simon.
There was the great concert in Central Park
After so many years of separation.
And then again separation.

Why? It is like where have you gone Art Garfunkel.
Similar to "Where Have You Gone Mrs. Robinson."
Relationships change, but when there is success,
Why change the wheel?
Perhaps too often ego gets in the way.
And what was, is no more.
And then there is nothing left,
But "The Sound of Silence."

Allan Mohl
Ossining, NY

I am a senior who has been writing poetry for about the past twenty years. I live with my wife in Ossining, New York, and I have three adult children and six grandchildren. Poetry is an emotional outlet for me. This poem evolved subsequent to a televised Simon and Garfunkel concert in Central Park, New York, in the early seventies. They performed to a huge and enthusiastic audience.

America

America is the name
of my adopted land and country.
This is a land of multicultural expressions,
a land of many opportunities,
a land of great challenges and solutions
and a land of beautiful landscapes
for discovery, creativity and realizations.

Yes, I am an immigrant
in this land and country
built by the effort, dreams
and faithful determination
of millions of immigrants
including our Native American tribes
that are the heart and soul of our country.

Together, we can preserve
our freedom, pride and dignity
as we continue to build and create
with respect, passion, determination,
kindness, compassion, faith, brotherhood
and sisterhood the American dream
for our next and future generations.

God bless America!

Jesse Castaneda
Los Lunas, NM

Jesús Jessie Castañeda was born in northern México. He came to the United States in 1956 and since then has resided in New Mexico. Jesús is the father founder of youth soccer in New Mexico, having started the first youth soccer league in 1972. He has broken three Guinness World Records: Non-Stop Walk (spring 1973), 24-Hour Walk (September 1976) and 24-Hour Basketball Dribble (September of 1996). He also walked across the USA from New York City all the way to Venice Beach, CA, in 1982, covering 3,192 miles. He was also an Olympic torch bearer in 1996. In 1994 he dribbled a soccer ball from Albuquerque, NM, to Los Angeles, CA, in celebration of the World Cup '94 in the USA. In 1998 he dribbled a soccer ball from Costilla, New Mexico, to Chihuahua City, México, in celebration of the World Cup '98 in France.

The Face of the Deacon

A young girl one night wanted her life to end.
So to a bridge on the river she went.
Death to her soul, the loose pieces would mend.
This world was cold, and her anger did vent.

A silent figure passed in the night.
Without a word, he spoke to her heart,
Only the smile from his lips came into sight.
From that kind face she could not part.

"What stopped you from you evil deed?"
"What kept you from the fatal leap?"
Only one look, was her only need.
The face of the deacon made her weep.

I pray to God my face will plant a seed,
To separate evil from good with a hedge.
May I supply someone's deep need,
To stop their fatal leap from a bridge.

Virchel E. Wood
Redlands, CA

Freedom's Value

It's really frightening,
more than I can say,
that somehow we might have
all our freedoms taken away.

I fear that I might walk up
to the church house door,
and read a sign that states,
"You can't worship here anymore."

I fear that soldiers might go
from house to house and say,
"We're here to take
all your guns away."

I fear that the right to vote
might be gone
and the government will decree
a dictator on a throne.

No one truly values
the freedom they had before
until the day comes
when they have freedom no more.

Rose Dyess Anderson
Ellisville, MS

Rose Dyess Anderson was born in Laurel, Mississippi, on December 24, 1941, daughter of James Lamar and Mildred Moore Dyess. She's married to Rushel Talmadge Anderson Jr., the mother of one son, Joel Alan Anderson, and grandparent of Trevor, Jordan, Joshua and Gunter. She graduated from Ellisville High School and William Carey College, completed graduate classes at the University of Southern Mississippi, and attended Summer Writing Institute at Alcorn University, Bill Martin Pathways to Literacy Conference, and Novel Ideas Writing Workshop at University of Mississippi. She taught school thirty-seven years in Natchez-Adams Public Schools, Natchez, Mississippi.

God of Love

They claim to worship God, these angry men.
They catalogue the things that their god hates.
An angry god glimpsed only now and then
Where never once the tempest-wind abates.
I would not worship such a deity,
For my God loves the world that He has made.
He has a measure of His love for me
Who never earned the slightest accolade.
My God knows love for every man and beast,
And He commands that we should do the same;
That from our greatest moment to our least
The stain of hate should never bring its shame.
So let me always serve the God of love
Until he calls me to my home above.

Paul Hall
Montrose, CO

I am a widowed eighty-two-year-old retired Army sergeant. I was born in the small town of Ingalls, Kansas, in 1933. I had a second career in the Colorado Department of Corrections, retiring as a lieutenant in 1993. I have written poetry since I was eight years old. I am a traditionalist, writing in the metered style of the old masters. I have published one volume, The Quatrains and Selected Poems of V. Paul Hall, *with Trafford Publishing. This poem shows what I perceive to be the difference between Islam and Christianity.*

I Fight It My Way!

Sometimes I am so lonely…
I read some books, do puzzles,
I call my family and friends
And loneliness just ends…

   Sometimes I am so scared…
   The news of shootings, wars and fights…
   I think of love and peace
   And fear does cease!

Sometimes I feel so lost
And can't make up mind…
I sing old songs of beauty
And find my thoughts aligned!

   Sometimes I feel so sad —
   Too many friends are gone…
   I pray for them, for peace and love
   And feel God's blessings from above!

Sometimes I feel so tired…
There is too much to do.
I stop and write a poem!
I'm fighting it my way!

Aldona Kairys
North Providence, RI

Remembering 9-11-01

Let's watch the parade!
The parade of 1,000 American flags,
  carried by 1,000 patriotic men,
women and children.
  Marching to the beat of the drums
and colorful drum majorettes,
  remembering the terrorist attack
that brought this great nation to its knees
  on that fateful September morn.
Leaving thousands of lives lost
  and thousands more mourning and grieving.
We have come back with an intense resolve
  to right the wrong thrust upon us
and to show the world that our nation,
  whose strength lives in the hearts
of its people, cannot be defeated.
  We cherish our freedom —
and live by the principles established
  by our Founding Fathers —
    we believe!

Mary Jo Urseth
Ridgecrest, CA

This has become an annual citywide event in cooperation with our Navy base.

Tribute to a Sea Lion

A large brown sea lion
  lies near the high tide line.
His eyes show death in stalking him.

Gray boulders surround his bed of sand,
  agates and jasper.
His majestic head rears as I approach,
  still life there, but it's ebbing fast.

A fine moss coating speaks of his age.
His gray head is held proudly.
What harems has he been master of?
What distant beaches has he laid upon?
His eyes survey the calves his seed has spawned.

Here he lies alone
His final resting place,
  this sunlit shore, flowing into eternity.

Joan Hunt
Lebanon, OR

The Final Curtain

He held her hand while she was sleeping
and thought, at last, she's at rest
All that kept going through his mind was —
of all the women I knew, she was the best.

Her skin used to be smooth as a rose
But now was wrinkled and old
Her hair had turned gray, where once it was red.
Her speech faltered, where once it was bold.

Act I: He looked back over they years just like yesterday.
In his eyes he could see her as she was as a teen
No matter what she looked like then or now
He still thought of her as his special "queen."

He fell in love with her at a very young age
They married shortly afterwards and had a baby
From then until now, he loved her so much
and treated her as his special lady.

Her eyes opened slightly — she gave him a smile.
He smiled back to hide a tear
Her hand went limp and with one last look
He knew in his heart, the final curtain is here…

Clata Fisher
Elizabethton, TN

I am an eighty-two-year-old widow living in Northeast Tennessee where I was born and raised. I moved to northern Illinois where I later met my husband J. R. Fisher. He served in Normandy in WWII incurring four injuries there. We later moved back to "Clata's Tennessee." I wrote this poem at JR's dying bedside. I changed the characters and pretended I was dying and he was left behind. JR, you are my hero — your "Sally."

Beautiful Boys

A beautiful boy, a bundle of joy, taken from her too soon.
A sweet precious gift, with little blond curls,
to whom she'd have given the moon.
Then God answered her prayers with
blue eyes and blond hair,
a gift from the Lord that's for sure.
One that looked like the last, from two years in the past,
a likeness that struck to her core.
A cool day in September became her surrender,
her heart she could never retrieve.
She made him her life and then came a wife
as sweet as the gift she'd received.
Jessica gave him her heart and right from the start
their love could not have been stronger.
Two boys their reward, a gift from the Lord
with Bobby's likeness and love to live longer.
April 28, 2013, we will never forget
as the day that our hearts became broken.
Not just once, but twice for the precious
lives of two boys conceived as a token.
We will meet you in Heaven someday sweet Bobby
and Michael will be there with you.
And then we'll rejoice and sing with a voice
that Heaven's angels could only ring true.

Brenda A. Monroe
Bridgeport, WV

This poem is dedicated to one of my dear friends, Jane Revard, and her two boys taken on the same day many years apart. As amazing as this earth is, I know the boys are in a special place in Heaven. Rest in peace boys.

The Constant of Change

Yesterday lanterns—today laser lights,
Dim lights and shadows, no blazing delights
Once only lean-tos, now building of steel.
Pray what to our eyes will our future reveal?

As we all look around us, more changes occur,
It happens so quickly it's almost a blur.
With mergers and products attacking all sides—
Technology goes marching in fast giant strides.

As I sit dazed, amazed at the wonder of all
A message once heard I clearly recall.
The speaker addressed us with voice very calm
And uttered this phrase which was almost a psalm.

If you want to survive in this new world of ours
You must picture the bird which follows the showers
And think how like him your life you'll arrange,
And sing as you challenge the constant of change.

Lloyd S. Foote
Tempe, AZ

I'm an old lady of ninety-one years. Writing poems over the years has been wonderful for me. I have three children—two boys and a girl—five grandchildren, and ten great-grandchildren. Our local papers have been kind enough to publish some of my work in their poetry corner column. I'll keep writing poems as long as I can. I work as secretary to the Clarksburg Council on Aging and have done so for seventeen years now.

Call It

Nine whole months and the day is finally here.
All the anticipation in the hospital room quickly turns to cheer.
"Call it, 12:01, a healthy baby girl,"
The doctor screams as he holds up Mom's precious pearl.

Who knew that tiny baby would need so much.
Sometimes all the screaming could be eased by Mom's touch.
Who knew how much joy that tiny baby would bring.
But eventually, time would change everything.

Fifty years later, and now baby's taking care
Of the woman who promised to always be there.
This time, the hospital room isn't full of smiles.
The family's faint tears quickly turned to piles.

She brought you into this world but you can't keep her here.
Everyone knows her "time" is near.
The end of her tunnel is finally lit.
The doctor sighs, "12:01, call it."

Melissa Johns
Walton, NY

Blue Versus Gray

Many Southington men would answer the call
To don the blue coats and head South;
Taking arms was new to these farm boys.
Fate would turn against many of the brave.

President Lincoln knew this was a divisive war,
Pitting relation against relation, friend against friend.
Plowshares were abandoned for rifles —
A mother's kiss, a father's embrace sent them off.

Men with horses joined the cavalry.
Men on foot were in the infantry.
Trains took the troops to assembly landings.
How could they adapt to this horrific war?

The war would tear apart the fabric of their lives.
The seasons turned and mounted into years.
When would their sons return on two legs,
Or a box fit for burial, or no box at all?

Southington's bravest fought on
Though they were away from home territory.
Goodness did defeat slavery,
With the muscles of good old farm boys.

Michael J. Michanczyk III
Southington, CT

No Regrets

Hawaii, the ocean breeze, the fragrance of blooming plumeria.
There I met the Marine, who became the love of my life.
Soon he was sent to Vietnam.
At mail call, they hung around to share the goodies I mailed him.
Then his tour in Vietnam ended.
He followed his dream to play music in Frisco.
Two years go by—then I said, "Don't call or come visit me in LA."
"Why?" he asked.
"I'm tired of waiting and listening to girlfriend problems."
The next day he called and said, "Let's get married."
No hesitation—I said, *"Yes."*
So he came and off we went to Vegas.
Seven years of bliss for me.
It's true, love is blind.
I didn't know he didn't love me.
But, no regrets.
Now I see I was his healing for his PTSD from his time in Vietnam.
He gave me the chance to know love—though only one-sided.
The second and third wives left him after one year.
Maybe, as after a year, he would quit or get fired.
For me no big deal. He was all I needed.
Penny pinching to survive—no big deal.
God gave me the strength to not abort and so I have two sons.
Jesus Christ, He is now the love of my life.
Looking back—no regrets.

Michiko Tokunaga Kus
San Fernando, CA

The Eternal Triangle

We are traffic
On the Eternal Triangle
Apex angle is Eternity:
Receiver and Sender
Right angle is Nature:
Incarnation;
Left angle is Spirit:
Great Provider to
Apex Angle: that which was Sender
Now is Restoration, Receiver:
Anima: Rex, Regina: Anima Divina

L. J. London
Shaker Heights, OH

Memorial Day

What do you remember Memorial Day?
Do you kneel and thankfully pray?
Remember those who came before,
And lost their lives in an act of war.
Or do you remember the living
And all that they are giving,
And what of the ones who carry the scars of war.
Couldn't we do more.

Dianne Mulcahy
High Springs, FL

American Poet

Poems

Vying for attention
Everyone wants some
Right or not
Seasons pass
Equally and intensely
Serious, sober and sad

Music is the international language
Unless you are mute (whale shame)
Silence is golden but lonely
Into each life music must fall,
Could there be anything sweeter?

Constance Warren
Detroit, MI

I'm a longtime life member of the Grosse Pointe Community Chorus and sing as a soprano. We just had dress rehearsal for our Christmas concert tomorrow, so I'm thinking music, happy times and friendship. I love to sing as much as I love poetry. They go together so well.

Us Three

Do you recall that long road running, running through our years,
   running through the good times, running through our tears?
Do you recall the darkness and searching for the light,
   like three hoboes running through the shadows of the night?

We traveled on not knowing, what laid beyond that bend,
   times I used up all my jokes to make you laugh again.
Still we kept on searching, not wanting to expect,
   that life was sometimes similar to a stone around our necks.

As you look back remember, all those plans and schemes,
   and the times we had nothing but a slow-moving dream.
Yet we never faltered, we never slowed our pace,
   for shining through the darkness was that smile upon your face.

Someday when there is left but two, for one the road has claimed,
   think about those three moths flirting, flirting with the flame.
For one must go prepare the way, leaving just your brother and you,
   remember all the times we had and how we always made it through.

Us three, us three, your brother, you and me.

Daryl D. Brown
Burlington, IA

Consulting Yah-Weh

Father God, I come to you with a petition and with
Instructions from your son, Jesus Christ, to use his
Name whenever I ask for your help.

I am in the midst of a conundrum I cannot understand;
However, I believe your hand is on my shoulder and you
Will guide me through the maze.

Help me in my distress as I traverse the road
You have set before me. Help me drink from the
Full, deep cup of faith given me for strength.

I do not doubt your judgment in this "detour" as
Your wisdom far exceeds mine. I know you see the
Whole chronicle while I see only a sliver of your plan.

Help me accept this task as your divine will for
A new bridge towards an ending goal. Help me to see
This "charge" through your eyes as one who
Prepares a route for his children to follow.

Rekindle my spirit so I see the steps you have
Prepared for me to walk safely. Help me complete
This new task so your will is honored.
Truly may it be so, amen.

Mable M. Guiney
Ft. Walton Beach, FL

This poem is written with symbolism explaining a Christian's struggle dealing with obstruction of his plans. It can also serve as a model to follow if one finds oneself in similar circumstances. This poem's Christian doesn't like the displacement of his own ideas and wrestles with resistance inside himself. At the same time the Christian remembers the report of the cursed tree with no fruit and the story of Jonah resisting God's will, and he decides a wiser choice is submitting to God's plan and asks for wisdom in coping with a new venture.

The Men in My Family

One Sailor, two Marines, one Army they so were
They joined without hesitation as it was their duty to bear
My father having to get permission as he was only seventeen
My brothers and ex-husband all at the tender age of eighteen
Proudly they served and not one complaint
Their motto was to serve and freedom to maintain
Faces of joy returning from conflicts to US soil with scars hidden within
Hardships, near-death experiences for battles they did not understand or win
They are my heroes, but yet they are humble
My father is now gone but the flag that draped his casket said it all
I knew he was watching from above in formation and standing tall
Those still with us struggle with issues but would give their lives if asked again
This country we call America they would fight for it and it would not be in vain
For the freedom we so take for granted was won by men like these
The color of their skin or their origin was not a question asked of these enlistees
Life in this country opposed to living elsewhere there are no comparisons
Let's be proud of this wonderful country and proud to be called Americans

Yolanda Orozco Mendez
Houston, TX

Pebbles Ripples Waves

Throw a pebble in the water.
You will see beyond tomorrow.
Then watch the ripples as they grow,
just like the seeds that you will sow.

Throw a pebble in the sea.
It joins the waves to set you free.
The pebble then begins to dance,
and then its rhythm is enhanced.

Feel the power of tomorrow
to rid yourself of passing sorrows.
Face each challenge on waves' crests.
Try always to perform your best.

Watch the ripples multiply.
They fill the earth and fill the sky.
God is that force of the beyond.
Embrace the force and form a bond.

Throw a pebble in the sky.
It sways and flutters and starts to fly.
It then becomes a shooting star
and guides you to your own lodestar.

Join the universal wave.
Its power always makes you brave.
You're happy then to know your role.
Fearless then to seek your goal.

Diana C. Etheridge
Merrit Island, FL

Diana Etheridge received her BA degree from the University of Denver and her MA degree from Simmons College. She is listed in Who's Who in America, Who's Who in Science and Industry, and Who's Who in the World. She is the founder of EDEA! Inc., the idea clearinghouse for creators and inventors, and Cybernastics, a fitness website. She published a delightful children's cookbook, Cook 'n' Rhyme with Kids, *illustrated by her daughter Juliana. She has won several awards for her poetry and been published multiple times. Her haiku was chosen to be sent to Mars!*

The Wind in the Lilacs

She sat amazed in the presence
Of the seemingly prudent professor
Who having instructed the pupils
On the prospects of the syllabus expired.
Since the hour had elapsed
By the time the teacher collapsed
All the students except for
Miss Alza Merz went to lunch.
Alza had a fear of amazement
And sat discouraged at this revolting development
This would affect her career, she knew.
The faculty would have to be
Reshuffled to take up the slack
Left by the tragic and untimely
Demise of the seasoned professor.
Hey there Miss Merz stroll around
The grounds until you feel at home,
Said the aging Dr. Bazzar,
Long time administrator.
And Alza did just that
For the next four weeks
From October 22nd until
The twenty-first of November.
Her hay fever having turned
The demure coed into a consumptive
Mary Jane, Her beauty of form and features
Attracted the male patrons at Saints Haven.

Charles Andrew Campbell
Montgomery, AL

I was born in Dallas, TX, on October 18, 1948. Growing up I liked to write short stories, take photographs, and draw. I graduated from my fourth college in 1973. In 1970 at age twenty-two, I did time at St. Anthony's Annex. It was like a dream vacation; I have fond memories of the time I spent there. After college my aunt had me go to a rehab center and I worked for Goodwill Industries as a sheltered employee until 1980. Someone there told me, "Heaven will never be your home." This poem is based on some true facts of my life, cleverly written in a fictional light. I always have liked the young ladies as I grew from childhood to old age. They were (are) the final and finest portion of God's creation. I thought growing up that one day I would marry a fine Christian girl and have children with her and have a fulfilling career, but that never came to be. God bless.

A Poet's Wish

Oh, if I could only have my fondest wish, the greatest desire of
  my soul
That is to spend all my days and nights writing poetry, that would
  make me feel complete, my life would feel whole
I'd love to be free to write poems about both happiness and woe
Poems that might be ranked among Oliver Wendell Holmes and
  Edgar Allan Poe
From sunrise to sunset, instead of toiling and working hard, my
  friends would probably locate me,
Drinking tea, writing verses, and sitting in the shade of a large
  oak tree
Or, perhaps I'll sit in a long wooden canoe on a quiet little pond
I would anticipate events yet to come, and reflect on days that
  have gone
Maybe I'll take a leisurely stroll in a field of blood red roses,
Conjuring up verses of rhyme and wit, while holding one of those
  sweet flowers beneath my nose
I'll take long walks on a beach by the seashore, collecting
  seashells and looking up to watch the seagulls in flight,
I'll sit in the sand, and listen to the pounding of the waves at night
These are all fantasies and dreams by people whose minds are free
  and clear to see
Humble, everyday people who write poetry, and dream idealistic
  dreams and have wishes, people like me

Alan Knight
Champaign, IL

Everyone has their own personal fantasies. And everyone has at least one favorite fantasy. I thought I would submit a poem about my favorite fantasy. I hope people find it inspiring and interesting.

Land of the Free

Liberty and justice for all, that cannot be
Not in this country where God has placed me
I must have a permit to fish or hunt
To build me a house or park for lunch

I can't light a fire or burn my trash
I must get permission, call someone and ask
You pay all your taxes on your property and pay
But how your money is spent, you have little say

The truth from the Bible we learn now is wrong
Not only do we say these filthy words
We feed them to our children in games and songs
And when you say the Bible is true
Those who don't believe, say it's not their view

You must not pray or put up a cross
And a manger scene at Christmas, well that's another loss
We teach our children that God is dead
So they learn to take up guns filled with lead

I wonder where our country will be in the years ahead
When our homes are not blessed with a mom and a dad
God bless America, we say in our land
But the only place he's always welcome,
Is on the dollar in our hands

We used His name in cursing and slang
And wonder why our streets are filled with gangs
Still God loves America, and so long to bless
If only we would love Him, and try to live our best

Helon Phillips
Cordesville, SC

Proud to Live in God's World!

I'm proud to live in God's world
And be here in the land of the free!
I'm grateful that God has made this land
For you and also for me.
I look up above and see the blue sky…
The rainbows and also the sun;
And I marvel at all of the beauty
That can be shared here by everyone.
The mountains loom in the distance
And stand so firm and so tall.
I'm blessed with all the four seasons…
Winter, spring, summer and fall.
I can hear all the birds singing
And wonder just what they are saying;
The winds blow upon me so gently
And leave me swinging and swaying.
I'm glad to be blessed by the wonders
That God has given to you and to me;
The world is so full of mystery
And unbelievable things we can see.
We are blessed to live here among them
Stemming from the Star of Bethlehem.
God's child was born in a manger
And keeps us from harm and from danger.
We are blessed to be part of His world
And I marvel as each day is unfurled.

Nancy L. Oswald
Gladstone, OR

I began writing poetry sixteen years ago after my husband's death. It has provided a healing catharsis for my aching heart. I hope to someday publish a book of inspirational poetry and a children's book of poetry. I have written the poems and just need to contract with a publisher. I am so very lucky to live here in America and enjoy all the wonders and freedoms it offers. God has been good to me in so many ways. He has given me two loving sons and daughters-in-law as well as four darling grandchildren. I have been truly, extremely blessed.

Truth

Your vodka solution
Releases the evil from within
The splash of lime
Offsets the acidity of your tongue
Stumbled sentences
The clinking ice
Mimics the violent spells she endures
Next round turns to eight
As she remains in her place
Tucked snuggly in your pocket
Far from sight, from memory
Empty glasses pile
Like blurred memories
Even afterthoughts get the dignity
Of being remembered at some point

Gretchen L. Gloff
Lawrence, PA

To Our Veterans

Tears and fears must flood your minds
  a heavy heart you carry

Might be a single person or perhaps
  one who is married

Courageous, unselfish and giving
  it may even be your life

And yet when orders given
  you take it all in strife

Away you go not knowing
  at where your task may be

You're striving to keep "freedom"
  so enjoyed by you and me

Dear God bless all our veterans
  in hopes they'll soon be home

At last their tour is ended
  no more battlefields to roam

Praise and thanksgiving
  we owe to you, each and every one

Three simple words convey our feelings:
  "Job well done"

Thank you!

Patricia L. Carstens
Oak Forest, IL

Missing Natalie

Lord it just don't seem fair
  To have one day, then not be there,
  A sister filled with care and love
  Now gone to be with God above.

We miss her Lord, and always will
  But Heaven now will get the thrill
  And share the special little sister
  That made us love her, and now miss her.

Life gives us lessons we must learn
  That God creates—then we return
  And now with God, it's a better place:
  She's in your arms, and in your grace.

So Lord we thank you for the time we had
  But now she can wait with Mom and Dad.
  And one by one we'll join her too.
  It's the plan God has for me and you.

Donald B. Perlinger
North Huntingdon, PA

If you have sisters as great as the four I've got, love them and pray to God, asking Him to let you keep them for as many years as you can—before he calls them home. Natalie was my tagalong when we were younger. I wrote this poem for her the day she died! She will have the first copy with her forever. I will have a loving memory of her in my heart forever and ever.

Proud and Strong

There I stood antagonized, a hostage
In disbelief of what I am witnessing
All in moment's notice our world falls apart
The debris, the dust, the unforgettable sounds
Piercing screams, the despondent grief
Instantaneous emptiness,
Overwhelming embitterment
Trembling, panic and terror set in,
We drop to our knees as millions of tears fall
Together into a mournful pool
Swiftly, out of the rubbish and dross,
Arising from the ashes, our glorious flag,
Proud and Strong
The weight of a torn nation
Rests on her stars and stripes
As the people of these great states unite,
We begin the arduous duty of saving strangers,
Putting ourselves in peril to find those
Entombed voices
With the red, white and blue taking wing in
Every household across America,
We will heal and persevere

Joann C. Martinez
Concord, CA

Keep On Keeping On

Keep on keeping on is the secret to
Healing of a broken heart
For we are not promised all would be easy in this life
From the very start
Oh, how nice it would be
If we did not have all these bumps in the road
But, Lord, I know now we have to be showed
That is the great lesson we learn
We gotta keep on keeping on
Or downhill we will turn
'Cause we know in our hearts
It is part of your plan
To help us grow wiser and stronger
Man or woman
If we just keep on keeping on

Pat Word
Vernon, TX

American Poet

The Calendar

I have a calendar on the wall.
It tells of winter, spring, summer and fall.
It has dates to remember,
All the way through December.
It takes three hundred sixty-five days to be complete.
Divided by seven makes fifty-two weeks.
Twelve months are named within.
The month of December spells the end.
There are certain days called holidays,
That we should remember always.
Each year they may be the same,
And we remember them again.
The calendar must be renewed each new year.
Then we can keep track of the years we are here.
It counts the years and our date of birth,
For the time we spend here on Earth.
There is a special day we count seven,
To keep it holy on our way to Heaven.
And when we take our last breath
It will show the date of our death.

Omar A. Walker
Bluejacket, OK

A Little Song of a Captain

From V. Lebedev-Kumach, music of I. Dunayevsky
Translated from Russian

A courageous captain John
Plowed an ocean on and on.
Many countries he had seen at each turn.
He drowned twenty times almost,
And amid the sharks was lost,
But he always kept his head and never boast.
   In mishaps and in fights,
All along he sang a song to be all right:

"Captain John, Captain John, make a smile, please.
For the bright smile is a flag of the ship!
Captain John, Captain John, don't forget this:
To succeed — a man must keep a sturdy grip!"

But once, traveling afar,
He had met a beauty-star,
And he fell in love, like plain boys — unawares.
Twenty times be blushed confused,
And turned pale, and was obtuse,
And he could not smile — for fear: she would refuse.
   He confused, was obtuse,
And there nobody had sung the song he used:

"Captain John, Captain John, make a smile, please,
For the bright smile is a flag of the ship!
Captain John, Captain John, don't forget this:
To succeed — a man must keep a sturdy grip!"

Emil Brainin
Pelham, AL

The Shadow Season

Speak not of love
When there is not hope or heart
To ease this bitter madness
  Where is the joy
  Where is the sadness
To ease the hour
To call upon some inner power
To flush away the pain
Out of this hour's despair
Down onto the shattered rocks
Or over heightened dreams
Into that murky flow
  Of history unclaimed

We blame the stars
When ancient long proclaimed
  It is not within the stars
  But our own souls
  That cannot choose between
  The dandelion and rose
When each are guardians of our memory

Donald Ransom
Detroit, MI

Freedom for the Free

I love America
It is my home
  with lands and waters
It is my country
  orchards of fully flushed fruit
  tracts of golden grain
  vine ripening vineyards
  farms and fields
  cities of towers and towns
This is the land
  to which my children's ancestors
  came on slave ships
This is the land
  in which my ancestors
  walked the Trail of Tears
I love this land
It is a good land
  but massive mountains
  of blood have been spilled
  much cruelty has been
  covert and covered
  and hubris has been
  high handed and hidden
This is my land America
May *all* people here
  always be free

Eleanor Shannon Lee Blakeny
New York, NY

Freedom Reigns in the USA

In the midst of darkness,
there is light.
In the midst of the light,
there is freedom.
In these moments, freedom
is our battle cry.
Freedom!
Freedom!
Over and over again, freedom inspires
dreams to come true.
In the name of freedom, many serve and sacrifice
for me and you.
In the preservation of freedom, many labor and die
for thee.
Give thanks to all the heroes.
Remember, freedom isn't free.
Freedom!
Freedom!
Freedom!
Freedom reigns in the USA.
Freedom is our destiny.
This is our land of liberty.

Pauline E. Blagrove
San Antonio, TX

Untitled

The love within me,
Leaps into the stillness
Of my empty soul.

Dancing along the ivory fields of love,
Knowing that true love is
Only a kiss away.

Take me where lilacs bloom,
And the golden mist
Of a velvet dawn,
Plays upon the golden fibers
Of my lonely heart.

Where our lips
Are joined together,
One last time…

To say

Goodbye!

Stephen David Hart
Ojai, CA

I was born in Pipestone, MN. I loved baseball and football and still do. I was inspired to write by reading Shakespeare. Thank you for printing my poem. My father was editor of the newspaper Pipestone County Star, which was in the Hart family for eighty-six years.

People Helping People

Looking up, I am not equal to anybody
Casting down my eyes, I see disadvantaged people
I am disappointed and draw a sigh gingerly:
This earthly life is very disproportionate!

More people bewail than smile to accept their lot
It is a perennially evident truth
People must have compassion for people heartily
In the midst of all creation

What can we do now
To reorganize our unfair society?
Each person should make one's contribution eagerly
To reform our people's unreasonable existence

Oh! People of capability and benevolence
Please join forces with one accord
To assist others' laborious human subsistence
Who lead extremely miserable conditions

People ought to help people
It is our naturally inborn duty
People should admire and esteem precious humanity
That is the warm and charming love lasting forever and ever…

Minh-Vien Nguyen
San Francisco, CA

Of Days Gone By

As I walk this path on a cold bitter day,
There are thoughts of my childhood
That I've tucked away.
My green knitted cap still warms this gray head,
And my old knitted mitts darned with various thread.
Saturday matinees at the theater in town,
My big brothers took me with them,
But each had a frown.
Saturday evening was taking turns in a tub,
Being scrubbed by Mother, she surely did rub.
Now off to the kitchen we trooped
For a bedtime treat, her homemade cookies
And milk couldn't be beat.
God bless my mother.

Shirley A. Zimmerman
Lebanon, PA

The Old Oak

Upon the hill a single tree
Growing high on the crest
Like a refuge it seems to be
And home to honored guests

The old oaks spreading branches
Hosts birds' nests where babies squirm
Open mouths awaiting their chances
When Mom brings that juicy worm

Welcome shade in day's heat
Broad leaves cool the summer day
A comfortable and airy retreat
Good place to while away

Resting against its large dark trunk
Taking in the distant views
Clears my head of all the gunk
And chases away the blues

Next time I escape the ol' rat race
And I need somewhere to go
I'll remember this special place
And a friend I've come to know

E. H. Barnes
Moody, OK

Where Has My Time Gone

Where has my time gone?
I am a senior and retired now — 93015 ago,
Sitting waiting for excitement
There are rooms to paint, floors to replace
Where has my time gone?
With speckles of gray in my hair
Now that I am a senior, life has changed for me
Forgetting what day it is — no longer have to be there
Time is still ticking for me to start to live
Where has my time gone?
It seems to have slipped away from me
Now is the time to live each day to the fullest,
Having fun, look at the sky! Beautiful stars aglow
With a giggle — no alarm clock — don't have to be there
Where has all my time gone?

Shirlene D. Williams
Palmdale, CA

In the Heat of the Moment

There is a time when coming to a crossroad of choice:
  to fly off the handle and react
  or to step aside and let the situation be as it is.

The moment may be a challenge to remain calm and collective
  when inside emotions run riot.

Instantaneously, the ugly monstrous head
  rears up to retaliate or destroy
  and blindly acts insane with fear, anger or rage.

Or the moment may be an opportunity
  to say to oneself: "Take a breath, count to ten.
  This, too, shall pass."

With the emotions subsided,
  the eyes of the mind are opened
  to do the next right thing.

The turbulent of being caught off guard
  creates the heart to pound and the breath to race,
  and yet the soft quiet voice inside
  begins to calm the nerves in the storm —
    peace overcomes the heart
    and stillness and serenity slows down the breath.

The minute time is fluid with acceptance, tolerance and understanding.

There is a choice. Which one will it be
in the heat of the moment?

Roger H. Dobitz
Sioux City, IA

Life is a journey full of many moments, and some of these moments can particularly stand out when a situation comes up unexpectedly. This poem is such as one. Interestingly, the pieces of the puzzle of the poem unraveled for me. I was "in the heat of the moment" when at work and I said to myself, "Hey, these words sound like the title of a poem!" The next day the poem revealed itself to me. This poem gives credibility to my awareness of my feelings. I am grateful for such moments like these that can teach me a lesson.

Peace of Mind

Living life to the fullest
Wishing upon an open door
To see myself in retrospect
Of willingness to endure

Life is a gift from God above
Bringing myself to an
Endless shower of love
On being on a journey to
Find myself in an entrance of hope
And a heart of golden gloves
Sparring to the test of life
Reducing my memories of fear and strife

We only have one life to live on earth
Accepting the goals of my self worth
I'm taking one day at a time
Hoping to find peace of mind

Colleen S. Johnson
Silver Spring, MD

My America

My America is an endless New York sky:
Trimmed with lines
That beckon long shadows along a sunset

My America is the whisper of a jazz scat
In the air, as
I walk on
Old, torn sidewalks: aged by cracks
No one
Repairs

It glimmers with the lost gold of
An age—shines in just the right light
On some cold winter nights,
In wide-eyed headlights

It is breathing, heaving:
Heavy-legged, from its
Long, ongoing
Trial—lit
By old house fires, blood draining
As it cries out
Hope thin

But this America, my America: will remain—
   egged on by scat and sky

Joli Schumaker
Rensselaer, NY

Solace for a Troubled Soul

A troubled soul on a brisk adventure,
   Seeking refuge from distress…
   Tired, struggling, distraught…
   Hoping for the best.

Suddenly, the morning sky offers solace
   As its beauty softens the blow.
   Wispy trails of color… pink, orange and gold,
   Across the pale blue sky, floating just so.

The heavens illuminated by puffy, peaceful patches
   Glowing of hope.
All of creation embarking on a tender journey
   To alleviate worry and fear.

Meanwhile, nature's palate breathlessly adoring here.
Compassionate forces console, embrace and grant strength
   To one seeking refuge and grace.

Appreciate the complexity of your existence.
   Forces creatively control the world's balance;
   Nature does not question nor resist.

For the tender comfort of the morning's brightening sky,
   Not a hand must man lift…
   So spontaneous and generous
   This unique gift.
The essence of man's soul and spirit revived.

Michelle L. Henkels
Bloomington, MN

Mom I Remember

Mom I remember your elbows upon the table and your hands over your eyes. But mostly I remember your silent cry. I was just a little girl back then, but it made me real sad to see you weep back when.

There was always a bill to pay, never nothing left for you the next day.

I remember how your legs would hurt, and your hands would crack and bleed, but you kept on because you had all of us kids to feed.

Making our lunches and no one wanting the crust, and how we all made such a fuss, but you would say it's okay, because you like it best.

I don't know how grateful my other siblings are for what you did and what you had to go without! But Mom I want you to know I remember. I remember everything back then that you did and even now!

I want to say: Thank you! Because Mom, I do remember!

Carol Williams
Sioux Falls, SD

I was born in Sioux Falls, SD, where I grew up; I also grew up in Colorado. I had six siblings and a wonderful mother who encouraged me to keep writing. I also have five children; one has gone home to be with our Lord. Writing has helped me express myself and also take me places I've never been, and religious poetry is very close to my heart. I like telling my story through my poems. I started as a child and never stopped. I hope you enjoy my poems as much as I love to write them. God bless.

Power of Love

When you are touched by the power of love,
You will feel something beyond your dreams.

True unconditional love is out of this world,
You feel this and cannot believe what happens.

The smooth flow of water over the rocks in a river,
Is the depth of love in each man's heart.

The fresh breeze sliding over your face,
Is the gentleness of what love is all about.

Feeling the power of your heart will bring a wave,
So powerful that you will be guided.

When you see the sun stream between the clouds,
Love is the warmth surrounding you.

Love gives you the wonderful experience of peace,
Letting you experience great gratitude.

Love is the answer to all of our issues,
You experience total tranquility.

Anthony E. Jordan
Palm Beach Gardens, FL

Our Brave Military

Committed at all cost
Sworn to protect
Serve our country —
Humongous challenges
Courageously accepted
Loved ones left behind
Blind with fright —
Many return manned for life,
Worst, body bags
A war fought for you, I
PTSD syndrome, nightmares,
Never subside, destroying lives —
Independence at tremendous price,
Let's remember every sacrifice —
Support "our brave military"

Patsy Violette-Hayden
Hermon, ME

Apalachicola Oysters

Have you ever eaten oysters
From Apalachicola Bay
Fresh from briny bottom coolness
Bringing tastes of places far away?

Hear the steamboats paddle wheeling
To Apalachicola Bay
Bringing cotton Liverpool bound
Taken then to places far away

Granite City, shimm'ring brightly
By Apalachicola Bay
Built from blocks for ballast brought
Sailing smooth from places far away

Lumber laden barges drifting
Through Apalachicola Bay
Vessels anchored anxious waiting
Taking wood to places far away

Eat your oysters chilled, enjoying
Near Apalachicola Bay
Watching net-winged boats out fishing
Harvest crops from places far away

Sure you've never eaten oysters
From Apalachicola Bay?

Caroline Steele
Harlingen, TX

Caroline Steele is a former X-ray technologist, mother, retired teacher, and hopes-to-be author. She enjoys history, and while enjoying oysters at a festival in Apalachicola, looked into its history. This poem is about the different time periods of this town in the Florida panhandle.

On the Good Ship Lollipop

I watched the Republicans at sea;
They each vowed hard and yelled, follow me:
Their voices became jumbled
And sounded like my Aunt Fanny,
And everyone thought it was funny!
  O it's *we* that are captain of this little ship,
Of a ship that goes wherever it pleases to go;
  And our ship flies it's flag proudly before the
  world;
And when nation is older, we'll set the democrats straight,
  how to run a country onto the shores of Deficit!
For we'll grow fat off of lean times, our ship
  will thrive on corporate offerings, and Iranian
promises, our ship, God help her, steering where
  politicians guide her; our ship
it's cost effective, sound policy, to bend when ill winds
  blow;
so tax the rich, and cigarettes, give to the middle class!
  O as far as you can see, nothing but lobbyists, downsizing
  and milking the cash cow of state!
We fund cancer research, uplift the rich to be richer,
  and bee demises explore;
O to land upon *no more* as never before,
  and as a last resort, show love for our veterans!
Offer speeches and bring forth traditional fail-safes!
  O it's *we* as *captains* of the good ship Lollipop!

Lonnie Bailey
Pineville, WV

Lo He Comes!

He is coming!
Lo He comes, He comes all glorious, lo He comes,
He comes victorious, lo He comes, yes, Jesus comes!

He is coming!
Those words have been preached to us
for so many years. Doubters, and skeptics, have so
foolishly broadcast, "It's coming out of our ears!"

He is coming!
While others have cherished deep in their hearts,
the balm those words have provided. I'm so grateful
to have the required faith, and know my Lord
will not suffer me to be divided!

He is coming!
One spectacular midnight, as the death knell peals,
a feeling of wonder permeates each saint as he kneels.
They spy the long expected token they have waited for
so long. As the small black cloud appears, first
silence, then it bursts from the trembling lips
of the throng: "Lo He comes!"

Royce W. Sappenfield
Ceres, CA

I borrowed these first few lines from that wonderful hymn as a fitting tribute befitting a king, King Jesus! How can you describe and lend justice to the magnificence of the most spectacular moment to ever sear the humble minds of a gathering of people on the verge of deliverance—not just liberty from oppression, as the grateful French citizenry and others greeted their liberators, the American soldiers at the end of WWII, but the final cessation of all that is evil in our world. And to know that we are going to Heaven! O precious Jesus!

Sweet Hurt Feelings

When I have hurt feelings,
I sit and wonder, "Why
would anyone hang up on me
And make me wish I'd die?"
But as I sit and contemplate,
A sweetness fills my soul,
Because I know,
In Heaven at last,
I'll be completely whole.

Janice R. Meyer
St. Louis, MO

I have always enjoyed writing. As a child, I would throw a ball against the wall in my yard and make up stories as I said them aloud. I always wondered if anyone heard me. Now, years later, I have been heard as I self-published a novel, A Rainbow for Ellie, *with the help of Eber & Wein. I am a former English teacher and reside in St. Louis, MO, the home of my birth.*

Imagining Heaven

In my bed 2:30 AM in the morning,
I am happy, it's my birthday,
The cool of the morning as the new day rises,
I sense Heaven's beauty in the far beyond.
I see that it is a mellow light, with peace and tranquility,
The air is mist and the flowers bloom
And the soft sounds of music soothe my heart.
I believe no one is left out if you accept the Savior,
Jesus visits us all, one way or the other.
I felt Heaven on the Great Wall of China
And believe many who helped built it are there too.
The great fortress walls of ancient Wuxi
Made me again wonder at the marvel of Heaven.
I am hoping that one day I won't be left out
From Heaven, for I have accepted Jesus as my Savior.

Wycliffe Tyson
Miami Beach, FL

Mom

A timeless beauty with incomparable style
An inner beauty in that smile
Immediately liked by all she meets
Rose's warm, loving way accomplishes this feat
Growing up was an enchanted time
She and my father created a world that rhymed
They made a home loving and bright
The artwork she chose was just right
Christmas Day was hard to believe
That peek around the corner was a magical scene!
Supper time was a joy in itself
Food that good couldn't be bought on a shelf
Slovenian is our heritage with comradery and good times
Polkas and waltzes on the button box are always sublime
She came from parents who were just as kind
To sacrifice for us she didn't mind
Worked in a factory during the war
Doing her part while Dad did his tour
Then an office and restaurant where she had lots of fun
Home to make dinner with more work to be done
Always fun with lots of jokes
Smiling and entertaining her four blokes
She helped through tough times with love as my guide
On wisdom and steadfastness I can always rely
How can I say thank you to one so dear?
Only return my love throughout the years

Charles F. Mateya
South Park, PA

Manic Depression

Three with two poles: euphoria at one end, deep despair at the other.

Merv convinces Bob that a microphone has been implanted
in his back.
We get there just in time to stop Bob from using a razor
to cut open his friend's flesh
and relieve him of the delusion.

A package for Merv at the front desk; he has ordered a tuxedo
to wear to his family meeting. It's what we remember
when we hear he placed a gun in his mouth
and pulled the trigger.

When Bob is transferred to the state hospital for long-term care
a limo arrives at the main entrance.
He wants to go in style.
Is this what he thinks the day he hangs himself
until dead?

Raven-haired beauty with almond eyes,
gentle soul and bright mind,
why did you slice your throat from ear to ear?

Did you fail to take the lithium, or did it fail you?
Was there something more *we* could have done?

Unanswered...

Lois Halley
Westminster, MD

Lois got hooked on writing at age twelve when one of her short stories was published in the school magazine. As an RN with a master's degree in business, it wasn't until she retired in 2007 that she began writing in earnest. Since then, her fiction, non-fiction, and poetry have appeared in numerous periodicals and anthologies. Twenty years of her forty-four-year nursing career were spent caring for people with mental illness. Although names were changed and situations altered to protect privacy, this poem is about three patients she cannot forget.

American Poet

Ruby

Please talk to me of Wisdom
   I will understand.
I promise not to judge
   If you place Her in my hand.

She is kind and gentle
   And always so profound,
More precious than the ruby
   In the belly of the ground.

The fruit of Wisdom should be seen
   Sought after to be heard.
Keep it, guard it, let it guide you
   It's in the pages of His word.

Please talk to me of Wisdom
   I will understand.
I promise not to judge
   If you place Her in my hand.

Maureen McLaughlin
Houlton, ME

Atoms

Floating particles
with unbound freedom
circulate in the universal air:
gathered and harnessed —
the energy of unlimited force.

We are but particles:
molecules of atoms — our brain
the atomic mass
giving vast potential
to harness and produce the energy
of a paranormal force — and
bring about
superhuman abilities akin
to the gods

Antoinette Goodlow
Union City, NJ

Rut or Routine

There are things I do every day
I like to do these things my way
I ask myself which style I'm in
A rut or routine, as I begin
A rut would have me stuck
Like a truck in a muddy ditch
Spinning my wheels, now here's the hitch
With mud splashing way up in the air
I work like the mischief, am going nowhere
Routine has more order so I would just know
What I should do and where I should go
Like a train chugging right down the track
Making regular stops, not looking back
Planning ahead helps avoid a snag
Because doing things over is really a drag
With routine I have a basic plan
Unexpected things arise so I do what I can
Some things are essential, some things would be nice
I write out my schedule and then check it twice
Expect the unexpected to confound the day
So I stay calm and face it, it'll be okay
Routine with wiggle room seems to fit like a shoe
Like sun up past nighttime sheds light on the view

L. Janeene Versfelt
Raritan, NJ

God (Doesn't Need My Help)

Jeremiah 31:34 KJV

God doesn't need my help
He's done all there is to do
He's gone so far as to forgive my sins
And He'll do the same for you

If you have a smidgen of common sense
And can grasp a fact or two
He'll show you how He set up the world
And why He did it for you

So go ahead and be thankful
Just call upon His Son
Because of His love for humanity
See what God has done…

John 3:16 KJV

Robert E. Brock
Hampton, VA

I'm an old man now (seventy-eight) on December 23, 2015, retired and enjoying life. My purpose in writing is useful to me and I hope insightful to you. I have another book (Expressions: Four Seasons) on Amazon.com. Just key in "Robert E. Brock."

'Til Death Do Us Part

Marriage, wow! Can you believe it? It feels amazing to finally admit
I can't ever "picture" life without you, so let me "snap" out of it
Somebody "pinch me," my "dreams" came true
My queen is gorgeous, sexy and beautiful, it was "natural" to say "I do!"
All that I needed in life God has given to me; Timing is everything
and I've waited twenty-seven years for this *"everlasting love tree"*
As we "grow," our strong foundation will "branch" together as one
Our leaves may "change" colors, and when they do, let's just shed "light" on each other like the sun
Communication, respect, and honesty are our "solution" to every "issue"
My "subscription" to you *never* expires, so *never* tears and *never* tissue
And even when temptation "arises" in the east of my brain, God "sunsets" my mind to the west; I've prayed for forgiveness my "whole life" and realize that I am not perfect but "I'll do my best"
My commitment to you means "more" to me than "life" itself
There are a lot of things that a "man" is prideful of, however, I promise to take that "ego" off the shelf
That's the "reality check," and after investing "with you" I'm ready to cash in; our "deposits" are permanent and we shall never "withdraw" from each other out of sin
"The Jones Bank" is full of "spiritual wealth" and through God we will succeed; God says "through sickness and health" we will have each other and "you're all I need"
I pray for our "afterlife" to be prosperous because "today" we are heading in the right direction; "I only have eyes for you," as your mind, body, and soul are my "only" affection
As I read this to you, I know I'm breaking down and starting to cry
I love you Jewel L. Jones! Forever and ever… until the day we die!

Artist Clay Jones
Fort Bragg, NC

This is my fifth published poem in two years. "Til Death Do Us Part" was written four days before my wedding. I recited this poem to my wife the day of our wedding as my vows. Everything I wrote, I truly felt inside. I cried as I uttered every word; I am a very passionate man. I loved my wife with all my heart and there wasn't a thing I wouldn't do for her. I pray that she and her family lives through the grace of God always and forever. God bless them and God bless those who believe in true love that will last forever and ever. Amen.

Than Queue

Set
Give
Gave
Lathe
Lathed
Portion of bending
Notion of bend—
Remembering the bending
While falling behind?
Were our people?
To follow a chance
Of the new beginning every new day—
Every day—
Save
Set
Borrow
Buy
Lend
How for with theirs?
And an answer to this?!
Of moments of memory of…
Is the question

Samantha Conrique
Hemet, CA

America

Whenever you visit America you will be
Impressed by the genuine friendship you see.
No matter where you travel to other places,
It's great to return to a familiar oasis.

Like a patchwork quilt America grows on you,
Such diverse nationalities, special to view.
Contrasting cultures you are permitted to see,
Congenial relationships and desires to be free.

The stability of America captures your heart,
And variations of the landscape the best part.
You can enjoy the vast freedom of space,
Open vistas and awesome skies to face.

Explore and discover vegetation at its best,
With a variety of fruits and nuts to test.
Many best kept secrets are available here,
With a relaxed, flexible lifestyle to revere.

Beautiful sunrises above mountains appear,
So when the sunsets the experience is dear.
America's panorama, a wealth of highlights,
When you mingle among us, gain real insights.

Life is like a vapor that vanishes away,
Each day a blessing; what more can one say?
Time to relax and enjoy America without fears,
Looking forward to enjoy the future years.

Patricia A. Amburgey
Wichita, KS

Half-Mast...

We didn't know them
Though they died for us
Amidst gun fire and missiles
Even children they could not trust...
They will remain heroes brave and true,
They protected this country for me and for you...
How many will have died, from the first to the last, all of them will wear it the
   Red
   White
   Blue
To cover their last resting place protecting me and you
How many more will die from the first to the last
Our flag was meant to fly for freedom not to hang at
   Half-mast...

Jacqueline Craft
Union Gap, WA

American Poet

I'm Still Standing

I'm less than my best, but grateful to be
Still standing and walking and able to see.
I've lived through some trials, disappointments, and tears,
But I'm still standing after eighty-five years!

God's goodness has blessed me
I'm healthy once more.
Still standing not bending he knocks at my door.
Again and again I can hear his voice say
Believe in my promises for I am the way!

Elva Dunham
Lodi, OH

I was inspired to write about the challenges of growing old. My husband and I celebrate our sixty-fourth wedding anniversary on June 21, 2016. Recently he was diagnosed with chronic lymphocytic leukemia and we are both cancer survivors. Through the years we have tried to focus on God's goodness and celebrate each day! We have been blessed with a wonderful life and are very grateful.

The Search for Gods

The gods in universe, men are searching
Until now no one found any footprint
Neither the snowy throne in the heaven
Where gods diffused the sacred actions

In the infinite space of a heavenly kind
Distanced the stars by million-year lights
The spacecrafts pursued with challenge
Lastly resonated just the non-existences

We just know billions of bright galaxies
Haven't found any planet for life or trees
Only some explosions of stars collisions
Gods only realized in a personal illusion

All men are free to have their own faith
Why to kill infidels like someone said?
Why to terminate the diverse believers?
Hoping souls will be near gods forever?

Why disturbing world communities?
Why disdaining human dignity?
Why defeating others without sin?
Though millions of men have a grin:
Consequence will boomerang to
Its cause!

Xaysouvanh Phengphong
West Valley City, UT

Since October 1950, Xay's (full name pronounced sign-sou-wan pan-pong*) poems have been published in "America at the Millennium — The Best Poems and Poets of the 20th Century," Great Poems of the Western World, Famous Poets of the Heartland, Our 50 Most Famous Poets, Great Poet Across America, and Our Best Contemporary Poets. There are two compilations of poems:* Unique Moon *and* Dancing Flame, *and twelve e-books of poems in Lao and Thai languages... Awards won include Great Poets Across America and International Who's Who in Poetry: Award Winning Poet, Poetry Gold Medal of Excellence, PoetryFest Poet of the Year 2015 and Hall of Fame Award.*

Missy US

My dearly beloved Missy US
In my heart I have molded an edifice for both of us
My love gravitated toward you from the onset
I promise you no drama, no concert
On the boulevard across the Charles River
Upon the germination of your ecstasy I shiver
I promise on my honor to hold my gong-gong to play
The melodies from my ancestral roots to make your day
Oh my sugar girl forever be my Miss
On Valentine you alone I will kiss
All my life for you I will sacrifice
Under our hat in the Gold Coast my mama taught me no vice
From Boston through Iowa to New Hampshire
With no one my love for you I will share

Raymond Obeng
Waltham, MA

The Gift

I will meet you there by the river,
some ugly morning at some self-chosen site.
I will bring all my past and what is left of my future,
and I will trade for your mysteries of the night.

This waiting has become tiresome for both of us,
and I thank you for giving me the chance to choose
the time and the place without the need to discuss
some tedious moral dogma or what I might possibly lose.

I will want to bring my classical music to hear
and you just bring your sweet, everlasting sleep,
some straight raw whiskey to chase away any possible fear
of unfinished business or a forgotten vow to keep.

I have been aware of you for quite some time,
many occasions you were near, others very far away.
Fast cars, Vietnam and motorcycles, I often crossed the line,
then disappointed you when I awoke to live another day.

But now your wait is almost done,
and I will not frustrate you like before.
So sit close beside me as I listen to Bach,
and soon I will give myself to you like a well paid whore.

Malcolm Lane
Camden, AR

Remember the Sorrow

As she sits before his casket
Her eyes…
See through a teary mist
Her cheeks…
Dampened by death's dew
Her lips…
Quiver as men "present arms"
She whispers…
"All this cannot be true"
"Taps"…
Clear notes reach skyward
"Day is done"
She sighs…
To soothe the ache
"Gone the sun"
Her hands…
Receive our folded flag
Remember the sorrow

Ariel Amend
Barnes, WI

The Actor's Gift

at a sky's request
assenting winds
unfold the role

of rainbow smiles
ringing in streams
courting colors
of Act One
Scene One
in spring splash
of mallard feathers
so landed
so coveted
in trust of trees
balancing light
on flourish
of styled steps
and orations
guiding arrival
of encore
fixed in seeds
on the way home

Michael Kirby Smith
Baltimore, MD

This poem is dedicated to Kirby Marvel Smith.

American Poet

Lily of the Valley

Lily of the valley, sing a
song of joy to me. Wake me
up with dewdrops across
the land so free. Bring
me hope, and purpose, from
across the sea. Be my
lily of the valley, my
bright and morning star.
Help me go far,
"lily of the valley."

Mary Deal
Sibley, LA

Love Is the Strongest Glue in the World

It is perfection
Toppled worlds and nations
The creator instilled that emotion in *all!*
Once it is felt…
Love is self-less!
Bara Avis new wave

Forty-three muscles in the face
Imagine the force of energy to smile
Starts and ripples as if music
Movies and jokes begin one muscle
To orchestrate a picture of emotion

The eyes have been a black stranger
Young innocent untouched
Saying, "Come! Do it to me! Do it!
Do it here! And here! And… here!
The *park* is now: *warm vacant ready;*
The leaves beckon to the *grass*, climb
The tree — it waits *incognito!*

Alyx Jen
Dallas, TX

Friends

We all have friends or acquaintances but only a few can be called
    your very best friend
They are the ones that will be there for you till the very end
You have spiritual friends who will always come to your aid
They offer prayers or guidance and their sincerity will never fade
Friends are a blessing, they come in all shapes or size
Some are knowledgeable and some so wise
Then there are some like a rainbow they have different hues
Compassionate or opinionated they have their own views
Friends are like the stars that twinkle from up above
But only a true friend shines with His majesty's love

Eileen Vigil
Walsenburg, CO

Say Something...

The words left unspoken
I love you
Don't go
I'm sorry
No
Yes
Forgive me
I can't
I won't
I wanted to
To accept the words that were never received
Needing closure, being able to move on, or to just begin
The what ifs, could haves, should ofs, that hung in the balance
A heated argument
A kiss good-bye
The waiting
Like a divorce, break up and even death, with no response to
   the cause
Silence being the final blow, but regret being the last one standing
Say something...

Denise T. Rosa
Charlotte, NC

I am a creative thinker. My mind becomes filled with words until I have no other choice but to empty my mind out onto paper. As an artist, painter, soloist, and writer, I enjoy using the gifts God gave me to inspire others.

A Fiery Little Beam

Today I went inside of me
Outside was far too cold.
I dreamed away the winter chill
In meadows dipped in gold.

'Twas sunshine of a different kind
Which lends these fields their glow
And gently warmed a frozen mind
Turned desolate by the snow.

It shone from where my heart is found
A fiery little beam.
Thus but one single ray of hope
Could make my whole world gleam.

Lisa G. Manning
Gloucester, MA

All children are experts at it, most grown up people have to relearn it: withdrawing into your imagination as a means of escaping the doldrums of a seemingly endless, dreary day. As a poet, thankfully, I am able to draw upon this too often neglected gift human beings are blessed with and have thus overcome many a dark hour. I believe in these "unpoetic, inhumane and technology driven" times we need to, more than ever, look toward the very young, to remind us of that eternal wellspring of hope deep within all of our hearts.

America Is Broken

No longer is the land I loved,
The red, white and blue
Its every color, every hue,
Not that I mind the blend we've become
But the actions of some
Have ruined our land, our waters
The eagle screams, our forefathers cry
To see our country lay in ruin
And watch our freedoms die
Yes, America is broken
We are now a token of what used to be
The land of the brave, home of the free
Can it be fixed, will it recover
Only if we turn to God to fix what we've done
The war will be long but it can be won

Sally B. Ray
Palestine, TX

Freedom's Pride

If dreams were a horse and memories his stride, down the
  trails of my youth I would again gladly ride.
To be free from life's frantic gait, enjoying instead the
  beauty of life in these United States.
To feel the wind in my face on a warm summer's day,
  the freedom to stop and explore each new wonder along the way.
We sometimes tend to forget as our youth fades away:
  What price is this freedom? Who has to pay?
We realize then that freedom's not free, but earned by
  those who wish it to be:
Our fighting men and veterans all,
The cop on the beat,
Our doctors and nurses,
And the firemen who keep our freedom strong and awake to
  any alarm to keep us healthy and safe from harm.
When the dreams of my youth come, once again I will ride
  down that trail where memories hide.
This time it will be with a new sense of pride for those
  who take a stand for freedom's call and make our USA
  the best of all.

James Harwood
Spencer, WI

I was inspired to write this poem because too many times we take our freedoms for granted. Without the courage and sacrifice of many brave people it would not be possible. I served in the United States Army from 1966–1968. I have six wonderful children, many grandchildren, and supportive family and friends.

Seasons' Dreams

Dream Maker, fashion my dreams for tomorrow
    So I may cast out my net and trawl—
    A weighty catch, far from small.

A desert sunset, silhouette of Saguaro,
    Capricious summer, resplendent fall,
    Oh hail Earth's bountiful seasons all!

Life's journey expresses our peculiar love—
    We laugh and sing in nature's hall,
    Because spring's beauty conquers all.

This illusory wondrous walk might I borrow—
    An elevated vision bestowed from above,
    Subdues this tempest on wings of dove.

An invigorating wellspring of joy and sorrow
    Emerges after winter's trying call.
    The vigilant carry on, pass the ball.

Melita Warren
Hays, KS

American Flag

The American flag,
Our beautiful flag,
It means so much to all of us.
It stands for freedom
And so much more.
So let it wave high,
For the glory which it stands.

And to let Betsy Ross know
We all understand.
When she made our American Flag,
She did a beautiful job,
With thirteen colonies, thirteen stars.
We have now fifty states,
In our United States.
And with our beautiful country,
It will always be our American flag.

Loretta Aul
Belle Vernon, PA

Linear Perception

When you're young,
Time slows down.
When you're old,
Time speeds up.
When you're in love,
Time is frozen.
When you're alone,
Time is stolen.
When you live,
Time is forever.
When you die,
Time is no longer.

Krisann Johnson
Richmond, IN

9-11 Remembered

Plane crash explosions through the air.
Now, united we stand awakened and aware.
Many good souls had passed away.
As the skies were filled with clouds of a dusty gray.
Now in the soft hours after this despair,
We resolve ourselves solid and make our moves and our prayer,
Wishing our loved ones, more than shadow, were there.

Derek Walsh
Millis, MA

Sad Oh No No Season

No Santa gifts, roasted lamb or ham
No honey or money for Aunt Pam
On this happy "holly-day"
Saint Nicholas I can't play
'Cause I've been scammed by Fake Uncle Sam

Ollie V. Zoller
Amarillo, TX

I was born February 16, 1931, near Reydon, OK, to Andrew Freeny and Cora Florence Saunders, ninth of ten children. June 2, 1952, I married William Eugene Zoller, WWII and Korean Conflict veteran. God blessed us with four children and two grandchildren. Bill died July 3, 1989, from a self-inflicted .410 gauge shotgun bullet through his hurting heart, ending his suffering on Earth forever, however, not ours (family and friends). This year, 2015, my ANB savings account was robbed by a fraudulent IRS/FBI group leaving me with no Christmas money, my reason for writing "Sad Oh No No Season."

Care

Did you ever look into her eyes and see
The stars that're there
Did you ever hold her hand and feel the
warmth to share
Did you ever hold her close to you and
Knowing the love within
Did you ever whisper in her ear how much
You really care
When you do, my friend, a life of love
You'll share

Gene Gordon
Webster, NY

My World

I want to tell you,
Red, white and blue
Are the ultimate hue.
Blood, purity and midnight sky
Are the only colors to fly,
And I will tell you why.
If I obey our laws,
I can champion any cause,
Even with all my flaws.
Where I live is up to me,
To pray and worship, I am free,
My choices are endlessly.
Mighty forces fight and die,
To bring peace for you and I,
Eminently here to fortify.
Perfection is not in our world,
Then we watch Old Glory unfurl,
Our minds change in a whirl.
Let's exalt our freedom now,
And never take for granted how
God, country and family endow.

Joy Dockery Randall
Bryan, TX

With all the imperfections in this world of ours it's still the best place on the planet. I am thankful to be an American. My faith in God and my country are what keep the rest of my world in balance. My glass is always half full and no matter how bad things get there are always better days ahead.

Vol. 1

(Why?) Can't We Love Each Other

Why do children God made in His
Own image think they are better
Than one another?
Why are we here on this earth?
Why do we make difference in one
Another?
Why are some of us very rich
And others very poor?
Why are we like a rainbow in color?
Well, until we as creatures
Made in God's image learn to give
Ourselves to Him, to fill that
Void in our lives,
We will continue to
Ask, "Why?"

Janie Aker
Calhoun, GA

I am a missionary called by God in 1981. I'm married to a wonderful man, Preston Aker Sr., and have three lovely grown children—Preston Jr., Matasha Campbell, and Rodney Aker. My favorite Bible verse is "Let us love one another." I am blessed with eight grandchildren and three great-grands.

For the Love of God

For the love of God
    Tell me what happened
        What really happened to the love
            You had for me
For the love of God
    Tell me what happened
        Where did the smile
            Go when you saw me
For the love of God
    Tell your desire to be near me
        And do not stay so far away from me
For the love of God
    Tell me did the stars in the sky
        Stop glistening and shining
For the love of God
    Tell me what happened

Bozana Belokosa
Pasadena, CA

Fool

You are your biggest fool...
Don't just get your hands wet;
Jump in the pool...
What is a safe bet... today?
Everything is controlled by computers.
Your life is at their mercy!
Hey! Go through the drive-through,
I'm thirsty.
Life is so fast paced...
What's really our place?
Does society decide this?
Or is it just a myth?
I'll give you a gift,
If one can just give me an answer...
To all this confusion.
People are so afraid—
No jobs, no money,
No home, no trust...
My mind is full of disgust.
Civil war is so close;
Gather up who you love the most.
The end of the world is so near.
Don't be a "fool"!
It's only God we should fear!

Gary Lee Scouten
Cherryville, NC

October

Oh! How bitterly sweet
you have become.
the past haunting—
the present uncertain—
choices painful—
reality clouded—
perception faint.
Yet!
Silent within the pulse
a longing cry
for faces touched,
smiles remembered,
love reflected,
on other days with other hearts
in loving memory
reminiscent by the magic caress
 of yesterday.

Nancy Taylor
New Milford, NJ

Common People Creating a Nation

When England was ruled by a king
And citizens were held by a string
That worked 'till men found righteous belief
And escaped by sea, ending their grief

Freedom in the Netherlands was tried
But their children lost their English pride
They found a ship called the Mayflower
That sailed the ocean with wind power

One hundred and two crammed down below
Cramped with odors for two months of woe
Then came the day when they saw the land
A wilderness waiting as if planned

Then they wrote the Mayflower Compact
A government by the people act
Leaders would have to be voted in
Their freedom of decision begin

They formed a government by consent
All agreed in this solemn event
A new land for the free to explore
New freedom for the rich and the poor

No privileged group controlled their lives
No one could take power who contrives
They all agreed this great location
No king will rule this newborn nation

Dorothy B. Fairfield
Merrill, OR

Grandma's Sweet Touch

An old brick house with a large porch swing
Where Grandma and I would glide and sing
Her sweet loving smile and gentle kiss
Her warm embracing hug, oh how I miss
That old woodstove, where Grandma cooked
I would sneak a bite though I know she looked
A little red tricycle for me to ride
It meant so much, my joy and pride
Grandma please, a penny or two
In her cabinet, she kept them, to a candy store I flew
In her many-room house we played hide and seek
In the parlor, I would hide as I told her not to peek
To her rocking chairs, we would go rest
A small child rocker for me was the best
A cistern for water, an outhouse out back
Only a simple house but never did we lack
Thick homemade quilts, feather pillow for my head
As I snuggled up, in Grandma's guest bed
Then she would say, it is time with a jest
Let God watch over you, while you lay down to rest
The memories I treasure, it all meant so much
How I yearn again, for Grandma's sweet touch

Sandra A. Young
Seneca Rocks, WV

One president that inspired our family and even the nation was John F. Kennedy. His presidency encompassed my early childhood years. One cannot view the Kennedy presidency without feeling a deep sense of family values. Truly inspirational is how I would describe the impact of the Kennedys upon my grandparents, parents, and myself.

H-O-M-E

H-O-M-E means many things to many across this land.
Some see how the Indians were deceived to steal their lands,
And treasures. Others see various wars from the Revolutionary
To the present day. Others know without a doubt that
"Being free" was bought and paid for by our sons' and our
Daughters' very lives.
Others see cowboys tending to a herd of cattle, roping, branding
Rodeos. Don't forget the dancing in the barns and saloons!
Others see great majestic mountain ranges, while others canoe,
Sailboat, rowboat, pontoon boat and fish in the Alaska ice and other
Remote locations.
Others see faces of our children, all beautiful shades, laughing,
   playing,
Working together as a team accomplishing goals "together" as one
Undivided unit. Elderly sit on park benches playing chess
   or checkers,
Arguing about their various religions or political beliefs.
Many others long for fame, however they can get it. It does not
Matter to them who gets hurt or not. They forget: "Love never
Hurts, love never lies, love never fails."
I am most blessed! I am loved. I have family. I have friends.
I have clothes, food, and shelter. To see them laugh, to see
Them smile is my dream come true!
There is nowhere else I'd want to call H-O-M-E than
My United States of America!

Rhonda R. Carden
Moultrie, GA

I thank Eber & Wein Publishing for giving me an opportunity to share with you. Mr. John T. Eber's letter talking about our USA inspired me to write this, along with all the men and women who sacrifice everything to keep us safe. What you do is greatly appreciated and is never in vain! Thank you!

The Tinkering Man

As a young boy he always had the urge to know.
He had to know the where and why as he'd grow.
He always had to take things apart:
To see how they worked and what made them start.

His over confidence always such joy did bring.
But, his talent wasn't in fixing things.
Instead it was in taking them apart;
In that he was a "master of the art."

"Guess he'll grow up to be a mechanic," they said,
As they happily tucked him into bed.
Little did they know or understand
He would grow up to be a "tinkering man."

"Now that I've put it together again
I think I'll take it for a spin.
Something is wrong with the ignition;
Seems there must be a part missing."

He would see the extra pieces lying on the floor.
He would then frown and slowly close the garage door.
"I don't know why it always ends this way;
What am I to do and what am I to say?"

Ruth Takano Sliger
Amarillo, TX

The Dance of the Grasshopper

This is the way it is today
And the way it will always be,
Ants labor and grasshoppers play,
Both want security.

"I have a plan," said the elephant.
"Yes," said the ass, "for the ants.
You can't see grasshoppers," said he,
"They never plan, they dance."

"They too, I'm told, will soon grow old;
Now who do you think will pay
For those who chose
To dance their days away?"

Rosemary McGraw
Anderson, IN

American Poet

Expression of Love and Compassion

When I first met you, I knew you were the one,
Who could fill my life with friendship, love, and fun?
The person I could love forever, until my life is done.
I thank God we're growing together and not apart,
Each day giving a little more of our heart,
Caring for each other from the very start.

Passion fire burns hot when things are new,
Our minds boggled with fantasies to do.
You're a person I could trust forever,
From the beginning I knew it was you.
You are a gift to me, and a present of an everlasting love
 and romance.

Each day seems to get better and better as time flies by in
 a glance.
Darling, my love for you will never be a game of chance.
As sure as time goes by, we'll get old and gray.
Therefore, I have chosen you as my best friend forever until my
 dying day.
An eternal love that's you and me, just the way it was always
 meant to be.

Fred Cato Jr.
Casa Grande, AZ

Patriotism

My husband was one of seven
  brothers who served in World
  War II at the same time.
For the family this had to be
  very sublime.

Two of these soldiers were seriously
  wounded,
But thankfully they recovered.

Their patriotic duty this family
  had paid.
It is one for the record books
  these men had made.

Carolyn Hurley
Thomasville, NC

God's Love

As I walk
in this life with the hand
and arms of the Lord
I see how little
and powerless we are to
evil, and how loved and safe
we are in Jesus' heart.

Annunziata Beavers
Lehighton, PA

Faith

Our lives are like a ship at sea
It can't always travel peacefully
Sometimes the waters become so rough
Fearfully we cry we've had enough!
Then only when we fearfully be
Then with our hearts we will see!
He will guide us with a beacon light
And always teach us wrong from right
He will calm the tempestuous sea
And let the waves unruffled be
Then gently lead us into port
To find the things we often sought!

Antoinette Italiano
Middletown, NY

God and the USA

I remember standing by my pappy,
Our eyes lifted to God and the flag,
Our hands over our hearts, chests
Filled with thanksgiving and pride.

Pap always taught us how blessed we were
To be born in the USA.
His blood was shed for her and us,
That we might live in freedom each day.

What has happened to our beloved country?
Why do we no longer trust God?
We get what we tolerate it is said.
If so, we deserve what we have as we complacently nod,

And, ignore the sins committed in this once great land.
Oh, what a heathen nation we have become in our self-will.
America, quickly, stand tall and pray,
And give thanks that our Father in Heaven loves us still.

There *is* hope for all in this grand old girl,
If we admit our wrongs and put Jesus at our head;
God will rally His *soldiers* and *saints* on Earth.
He will save us from Satan's power just as the Bible has said.

B. Kay Stephens
Bessemer, AL

X

X marks the spot
X on the window
X calls for you
I call for you

I call for you
You guide me
You are special
You are unique

You make me think
You give me hope
Your answers give
More questions to me

I call for you
X calls for hope
X calls for answers
You are X

Ann Marie Petrizzo
Hazlet, NJ

Never Forget 9-11

I see two enormous buildings
Their overwhelming heights
Touching the Heaven above
Quietly standing amongst the clouds
These monolithic symbols
The cradles to hold its humans
Of all colors and beliefs
As they busily work away
Not knowing today will be
The awakening of the giant within
That arises our spirit light
God has blessed America
Our courage that helps one another
Setting aside who or what we are
Becoming a family of brothers and sisters
Our freedom is that love
We share and die for
This light of my spirit
Will live forevermore
And I will let it shine all the time
Thank you God for our blessings
As we have come together
And never forget 9-11

Eufemia Tatham
Lancaster, CA

The pen is the palette in words that paints the story on the canvas. In writing, as an artist would paint his or her picture for those to view and enjoy, the poem becomes the finished picture in words that might warm your soul or make you smile. Today holding in one's hand is the evidence the book that can't be deleted, as you know a computer can erase the very words you've written. Our book of poetry becomes the ancestry to live on.

Tick Tock the Clock

The clocks go around and around.
So fast the minutes, seconds, speed
flashes like a light.
Sometimes it's gone in a flash.
Remember one thing,
hold on to the hour
hand and don't let go.
The circle is splashing in all our faces.
So clear your eyes
out before it's too late.
Help those who need your hand.
Forget the clock
it's not your fan.
Try hard not to fall.
Pull yourself up in spite of it all.
Let no one stop what you must do.
You will end up the fool.
No more slipping and sliding
down the hall.
Keep your eyes on that brass ring.
Sooner or later you'll grab that thing
Tick tock the clock.
Don't let people say you can't reach it.
Spring from the roughness of this life.
Believe it or not you'll beat the strife.
When life drags you down,
Stare right back and you'll be found.
Stop following around.
Life will grant what you need,
You're not a weed, you're a flower.

Eleanor Pearl Atzert
West Palm Beach, FL

My Answer Came

As I lay in my bed, so many things run through my head
I wonder, how we could be called daughters and sons of the most high king
That is so amazing to me
The marvelous one answered and this is what he said
I love everyone — yes even you — so very much and I had to do what no man or woman on earth could ever do
I sent my son to take those terrible beatings and the nails in his hands and feet just so no one would be lost
So now my precious ones, it is now up to you — I've done what I had to do
So please don't miss your chance to be my daughter or my son
I'm waiting to hear you call on me so I can write your name in my lamb's book of life as my daughter or my son
This was my intention when I sent my son on the cross
I don't want any of my children to be lost
Now my mind is resting and I say my prayers with a loving thankful heart
Thank you father for your precious son and I will do my part
Now I lie here with visions of Heaven in my head and I am at peace because I see you sitting there on the throne and oh how beautiful to know
One day I will see you and get to sit at your feet and give you praise and thank you for what you have done because I have become a daughter of the most high one

Anna Richard
Taylor, MI

To the Artist in Us All

Come with me to touch the sky
To capture a moonbeam as it wanders by
To encapsulate a rainbow in an arch of words
And release it in a flutter of birds
Come with me to marry imagination with rhyme
To travel forward and backward to rearrange time
To engrave a word picture on canvas, marble, or wood
To harmonize in symphony the magic of good
To rhapsodize fear, terror and wars
To show the integral battle of seas and shores
To immortalize a person, creature or place
Illustrating it within a paper's space
Come gather the wind, internalize the sun
Give voice to the voiceless and teach your heart to run
Art never inquires of the hesitant eye
It just reaches out and touches the sky!

Paula Compo-Pratt
Westville, NJ

Oceans Between Us

In the struggle for power
sometimes on the battlefield
where shifting sands of time
say a foundation for peace
can't be built
with only oceans between us
nothing would separate us
from people who want to bring
something to America's table
we wouldn't have to settle
for the crumbs
left by war

Roy A. Smith
West Columbia, SC

Thank You Father

Thank You Father for the beauty of the earth.
   Your creations are uniquely beyond equal.
The splendor of all forms of life is spectacular
   and truly challenges man's thought and philosophy.
Thank You Father for life, and time, and for creating me
   to be a part of this beautiful magnificent existence.
From sunrise to sunset, and vice versa, I marvel at the scene
   and all activity in between be it during dark or light.
Thank You Father for breath and those senses which allow
   me to participate and enjoy Your divine environment.
Thank You Father for the sweet and the bitter in life
   for it has and continues to provide a way for learning
Thank You Father for the Holy Spirit who teaches me to
   make intelligent decisions while interacting with others.
Thank You Father for the love of Jesus Christ
   and the many valuable lessons He shared with mankind.
Thank You Father for the word and its presence, and
   thank You for communication and your responses to
   my seemingly insignificant requests.
Thank You Father for being God the Father Almighty,
   creator of Heaven and Earth and all that is about.
Thank You Father for Your grace and mercy, Your abiding
   love, and Your everlasting forgiving manner.
Thank You Father for continuance and Your molding anew.
Thank You Father for the ultimate of gifts, life forever, love,
   Jesus Christ, and being born in Your image.

Ben Wilson Jr.
Uvalde, TX

We the People

Are we really "We the People"? How do we each answer this
 question?
Our country is free because of "We the People." Many have died
 for all of
us in wars we should not count but must.

Today we have become afraid of the unknown, and yet we stand tall
for we are "We the People." Not all have lost loved ones in wars,
or on the streets of New York, Boston or Chicago, but we have all
lost in the end.

We raise our flag at football and hockey games and sing proud
and loud our country's song, but we forget who "We the People" are.

We are the cop who walks his beat no questions asked, or a
 nurse who
can't stand by while someone is hurt in our streets, or a minister or
priest who marches for "We the People."

Those words are powerful for each of us, but never forgot it is
each of us through our own daily lives that make up "We the People."

Anne DeFrier
Elgin, IL

American Poet

The Red, White and Blue

I really enjoy the Fourth of July
To see the sparkles up in the sky
I thank the Lord our land is free
And that I live in *this* country

We have the freedom to say our peace
To own our land and to make increase
To love our neighbors and to stand strong
To forgive, overcome, and keep going on

I think America is the *best!*
She's number one among the rest
So if you ask me what I'm going to do
I'm going to *praise God* for the red, white and blue!

Shalom Christina Zoë
Roswell, NM

Zest for Life

I look around to see
The busy honey clover bee
Pollen falling from the trees
Broken glass and litter all around
My heart is heavy, my stomach weak
I've lost the zest for life

Teacher and children singing under a tree
Instead of a smile of envy
For their youth
I look with a heavy heart
Pity for the long trek
They must take
Happy at times, tears forever after
I've lost the zest for life

Not one but many tears roll down my cheek
Dear Lord, I'm ready
Is this the way you created it
Happy in youth, with age it dwindles
Yes, I'm ready, I've lost the zest for life

Betty Shlepr
Melbourne, FL

Ageless

He was lanky, tall, modest.
Someone who gave his best.
He used humor as his sword
to find success, for reward.

Few knew his hidden talent,
he had a very charming bent.
Self-educated to a degree,
not one to avoid repartee.

Growing with keen insight
to become a lawyer erudite.
He never drank or smoked,
and hunting, not allowed.

Reading and lecturing gave
the power to be extra brave.
His pleasing ways did ensure
an election to the legislature.

And next he tried for Congress
where he met with big success.
Then he served the nation
as president Abe Lincoln.

Gordon Bangert
Vail, AZ

Is It Knowledge You Seek?

A quest for knowledge, a thirst all carry along.
Some achieve greatness, power — prove they are strong.
But all can agree, "Ignorance is bliss"…
So if one is satisfied, what have they missed?
Look deep in oneself, all can seek the truth
If one is willing to accept all the proof.

There is a clear difference between being heard,
And simply listening, like to the coo of a bird
We hear its chirps, its howls, its cries.
But few understand all the bird's "whys".
Much more important it is — and difficult, too,
To accept the burden is not easy to do.

Feel good about knowing? About seeming aware?
But in heart of hearts, only few truly care.
What do we know of what happens there?
When trapped in our ignorance, there's comfort to spare.

Knowing and understanding are two different things.
Once one understands, ignorance stings.
It allowed us to avoid: shame, fear, and sacrifice
But now, fueled with empathy, we all pay the price.
A small price to pay. In fact, it is free!
Care, speak, learn, act, try, love, plea.
People know about tragedy, domestic and far.
In terms of understanding, we must raise the bar.
A quest for knowledge is all well and good —
But how much better it'd be, if we all understood!

Katherine O. Flower
Somerset, NJ

The Anguished Call of Freedom

She flows determined and as a stream unchained,
From peoples of many nations claimed.
Intercepting as an unsuspected storm unrestrained,
And ministers to all brethren as a preacher ordained.
Freedom's call cannot be contained.

She runs forward from deadly violence and stifling fear,
As cunning as a fox and swift as a deer.
She is sweet like honey and strong as a steer.
Her message, can you feel, can you hear?
Freedom's call is loud and very clear.

She glides wingless as a tantalizing breeze.
For freedoms, many have risked life overseas.
Peace and religious freedom the brethren wish to seize,
Along with dreams to dispel the evilness disease.
Freedom's call shouts for all, if you please.

She is comforting and like a loving hug.
Her prevailing spirit soars in a weightless mood, happy and smug.
She feels cozy inside as a bug in a rug.
Do you feel fresh oxygen instead of a suffocating club?
Freedom, most certainly, is the miracle drug!

B. J. Boal
Des Moines, IA

Talking to You Makes Me Feel Good

Since you went away, my life is so sad
You were the most precious thing I ever had
I thought all the tears were for you because you died
Now I know it was for my loss of you that I have cried
The days are long with no happiness
The nights are longer in a bed full of emptiness
I talk to you every day to tell you the news I got
I don't know if you hear me or not
Sometimes I don't know if I should
But talking to you makes me feel good
I get a lot of help from our son and his wife
They keep me laughing in this sad part of my life
I will talk to you again tomorrow
Hopefully, with a little less sorrow

Chester Williams
Jewett City, CT

Between Stimulus and Response

Life.
We're all human, aren't we?
So, how do you live your life?
What's your response to stimuli —
Hostility or kindness?
Callousness or gentleness?
Suspicion or trust?
Deceit or truthfulness?
Confrontation or peacefulness?
Meanness or goodness?
Retaliation or compassion?
Vengeance or forgiveness?
Rudeness or self-control?
Depression or joy?
Hate or love?
Out of indifference to others do you —
Demean them?
Dishonor them?
Shame them?
Condemn them?
Push them away?
Or, do you practice the biblical fruit of the spirit?
Remember treat others as you want to be treated.
For surely, what goes around, comes around.
After all, we all are human!

Bill M. Watt
Fayetteville, NC

I didn't grow up in a Christian home, but I became one as an adult. A dear friend once said, "You aren't the best Christian I know, but you work at it the most." It has been a lifelong struggle trying to walk the "narrow path" that Jesus talked about. As a daily reminder on my desk computer is a sticky-note listing the nine elements of the biblical fruit of the spirit which I try to live by daily.

Fabric of Life

As the sun rises in the sky, the colors of
thread on the masterpiece of life reflect
in the fabric of beautiful stitches of color.
Ivory and purple unite a family. The
lakes of blue surrounded by grassy
greens bring forth stitches of snapdragons
smiling faces blowing in the wind.
Bright stitches of red and tan remind
you of a son. Daisy flowers of pink,
violet and lavender, embrace little
girls dancing over the hills of covered
blossoms on the bushes and trees.
These blossoms are of rust and lemon with
glints of gold shining through. Each
thread of color is a part of life we
have lived. Shining dewdrops of love
on gilded lilies, sprinkled with silver
and gray as we grow older.
Now on the fabric there is sunflowers of
happiness with in gold with brown centers
and long tall greenish stems. Times of trials
and heartache are small stitches of black.
Clouds above float across the silvery sky.
The moon appears as a ball of fire, bright
and glowing an orange red.
Our life is a God-given pattern.
Choices we make become short or long
stitches of color. Life is a beautiful
piece of fabric woven by each of us
in the eyes of God.

Roberta E. Drebes
Quincy, IL

Purty Haven

The blistery cold of 2015, a dream surely seen
A grove of mighty bur oak, marked and ready for the axe stroke
One by one they fell, for they would make good timber beams
For by their growth rings, I could tell, this was one of my pleasant dreams
Cut and squared the old fashioned way, makes a man know he worked all day
The adz, the broad axe, and the axe, these will shape my cabin, these are the cold hard facts
When spring arrives, I will start, for love you know comes from the heart
With the footing poured and the rocks laid, this will make a permanent grade
The sub-floor and frame, timber made, tons of wood, if totally weighed
The carpenter builds, to defend from wind and weather, so frame it strong, to keep it together
Sheathed with red elm, a roof of cedar shakes, finished with porches, that's all it takes
Then offer it to God and St. Joseph too, bless it all, it's the right thing to do
For a modest cabin, simple but sweet, finds a place in my heart, that's hard to beat

Patrick L. Patterson
Mt. Hope, WI

The Flag in the Road

As I walked along under a gray, cloudy sky
A bit of red, in the road, caught my eye
Just then a car pulled to the side
A young man got out and ran up beside
He gathered the cloth and went to his car
Spread it out on the hood and brushed off a star
More stars, and stripes, the red, white and blue!
Our freedom — many have died for you
He folded the flag in a triangle true
Just the way we are all taught to do
He stood, saluted, and then he sighed,
"Respect for you, dear flag, will not be denied!"

Kay Ricketts
Bernalillo, NM

My Best Creation

A beautiful picture
I wanted to create
And in a flowery garden
Immediately I was

My dream became
A splendid reality
Because my Lord joined me
With three smiling little creatures
That to my soul enchanted

I took pleasure
And with emotion I smiled
Because I was chosen
On this canvas
To paint and to mold
In you I will set my confidence my Lord
That for a long time
You, my picture will conserve

Nieves T. Nouel
Boca Raton, FL

The Sound of Liberty

Within the heart, an inner voice,
Divine urgings in the soul:
Each person having special worth,
And each, a special role.

And Gutenberg was born;
Technology shaped the world;
Then everyone could hold a book
And read the sacred word.

As individuals, all could find
The truth, each for himself,
And measure with each mind
And heart, the wisdom of the world.

Democracy was given birth
With human rights and human worth:
A constitution, not a king,
A bill of rights, a liberty bell,
And all could shout, "Let freedom ring."

The liberating sense of liberty
Is felt within the soul,
And all enslaved by tyrants
Still hope, and trust, and pray:
Sensing something stirring and dreaming of *someday*.

Kenneth Swan
Marion, IN

American Poet

End of the Road

When I found at the end of the road, that I could no longer
 function as a human being,
I thank you God for this most amazing gift of life that you gave
 back to me
I was walking around blind and could not see
because, I thank you God you gave my sight back to me
I bend my knees in prayer and meditation
because it's an awfully good sensation
I thank you God because you are most high
I thank you God because I no longer want to die
I survived to live the treasure
of those who gave the last full measure!

Jennie Selby
San Diego, CA

My Choice America

I listen to friends
   Talk about the news.
Everyone has
   Their own different views.
Things seem to be changing
   In negative ways.
We're told to think positive
   As that attitude pays.
Does just thinking positive
   Deal with the truth?
To have positive changes
   Don't we need to see proof?
After I listen,
   I say to myself,
"I wouldn't want
   To live anywhere else."

Carol Kaufman
Portland, OR

Precious Life Lost

Once a simple piece of lead
caught creation's eye.
A plan was put in motion
to ask the question why.
It followed an assembly line
by the skilled worker's hand
and became a useful bullet
only loved by man.
Will you add meals to plates
or save the troops in war
or perhaps give fain warning
to a burglar at the door?
The maker held it proudly
and wondered of its range.
No one could have ever guessed
the lives that it would change.
With a self-inflicted wound,
my husband played a part
in taking my best friend,
my companion and my heart.

Dea Floyd
Monroe, VA

Campaign Kitty

Campaign kitty finds election headquarters inviting.
She hides beneath a worker's desk
And dreams of Morris' congressional knighting.
He is a national favorite among the furry set,
And not just among fun loving jet setting pets.
If only she too had the celebrity to become cat of the hour.
She would do great things.
She gazes at Morris' portrait pasted across a can of filleted tuna.
Campaign kitty tries to forget the human political agenda.
She embraces the unopened can of Morris' favorite kitty brand:
"Four legged friends must be heard," she thinks
As a woman opens the can of tuna for her.
"Even though man's political agenda is one of awe it has flaws.
National kitty polls show Morris ahead but I could do better,"
She meows.
Then with a consenting paw she puts the half eaten tuna aside.
She jumps upon a human candidate's campaign table and meows
    as if to say:
"Tell the human majority:
There will be no more overcrowded shelters or relegation to places
Where life is quite unfit and unrefined for animals of any kind."

Gail Logan
Macon, GA

Animals play roles in all my novels: The Sundisk, Time Is of the Essence, *and* A Matter of Loyalty, *available at Amazon and on Kindle. In other genres, my poem "The Mourning Dove" won World Poetry Movement's 2012 Best Poet's award.*

The Sands of Knee

Knee!
Knee,
what the hell are you doing to me, knee?
Knee, the sounds you're making. Knee!
The crackling, the popping, the pain, knee?
You have turned out to be my Achilles' heel, knee.
Given by parents, genes from their ancestral knees.
Knee, heal thyself. I place my hands upon you, knee.
God's same hands that once healed the leper's knee.
Him who gave me life and made you part of me, knee.
Knee, make yourself whole once more, knee,
so, I may walk among your uninflected brethren, knee,
like those whose lives lived without challenge, knee.
But, I have often challenged you to the fullest, knee.
On mountaintops, I've sung your praises, knee.
Knee, are you listening, knee?
In desert sands you pressed me onward, knee.
Through ocean seas, your agility I trusted, knee.
In flight you guided me, straight and true, knee.
Now life and time grow close to waning, knee.
Knee, you're needed now and appreciated more, knee.
Now, more than in my youth, knee.
Now, more than through all our times of trial, knee.
More than all these years we've spent together, knee.
Are you listening, knee?
Knee!

Hugo T. William
Eugene, OR

If Time Stood Still

Sometimes I wish that time would stand still
I know it is foolish because it never will
But I cannot help but wish it so
Since some moments are so harsh you know
The pain of loss, of war, of cost
The moments when you just feel lost
The times of happiness and moments proud
Of love, of achievement, and cheering so loud
I know it is foolish but just stop and think
Of the things you could change in the space of a blink
The horrible moments stopped, the pain we could erase
If only time would stop, so we could change that space
Tell me why time moves on, never caring with its song
The world turns, dreams forgotten, filled with tears
As I watch the changing of the years
I see many faces every day
Sometimes it is hard to look away
Death and fear, love and loss
These are always such a vicious cost
But less compassion and more of selfish greed
That seems to be a prevalent seed
I wonder often if people will see
Just how much we have lost, without the kindness to be
Sometimes, I do wish that time would stop
Just for a moment, on every clock

Heather R. Worley
Moclips, WA

My American Anthem

I will sing my American anthem,
Of this land of my humble birth,
Of all treasures this land offers to me,
And to all those that value their worth.

I will sing anthems to all our forefathers…
Forging a nation with parchment and ink,
Of a declaration of our independence…
From a land we were steadfastly linked.

I will sing of justice in our Constitution,
That strengthens the laws of this land,
And, of our freedom to worship the way that we choose,
And follow God's written commands.

I will sing of our flag, and give honor…
To all who defend it with pride…
And, I'll comfort and rescue those left behind…
That must face the oncoming tide.

I will sing anthems to sweet Lady Liberty,
And for all those she welcomes in:
For the rainbow of nations, language and creeds,
All sizes and colors of skin.

I will sing praises to our God for these treasures,
Secured for you and for me.
And, my heart will dwell where my treasures are found:
In America… the land of the free.
Yes! My heart will dwell where my treasures are found:
In America… the land of the free!

Ann Marie (Sandy) Forshee
Henderson, NV

12-25

Snowflakes of paste and glitter.
A paper blizzard.

Faux pine.
I sneeze otherwise.

Some assembly required.
A long nap by the fire.

A couple more cookies, another small crime.
Santa has long since made up his mind.

"Take the batteries from the remote control!"
I grab your hand for a winter stroll.

You remind me of a December sky:
As pretty when you storm as when you shine.

I'll try to keep you warm, but I'm only a man.
Throw two pairs of gloves on those hands.

I saw Christmas lights reflect in your eyes.
I saw the next fifty years as snow filled the sky.

Michael David Sterczala
Camden, MI

America My Home

We have the Statue of Liberty
  and the Vietnam Wall
We have the freedom to vote
  so come one and all
Our soldiers go fight
  to keep us all safe
So Americans stay free
  in this wonderful place
Mount Rushmore is a monument
  of four presidents past
It's a sculpture of stone
  and forever will last
We've had terror attacks
  that made two towers fall
That day in September
  we will always recall
We will never forget all the lives lost that day
Protect us dear Lord
  is what I always would pray
We can go where we want
  and do as we please
We can visit our loved ones
  who live overseas
We must all stand united in America you see
Because freedom for all is the way it should be
Pride will be something
  I will always hold dear
God bless America so there will never be fear

Peggy Lanese
Chagrin Falls, OH

I live in Chagrin Falls, OH. I am a mother of two and a grandmother of four. I live in a log cabin and I write poetry because it lets me put my feelings and thoughts down on paper to be shared.

US for Us

You ask me a simple question:
"What is freedom for you?"
This question creates deep flow of spiritual reflections
from soil bottoms to cosmic wonders of my existence.
I travel through the political systems, religious, nature
and observe a small oak tree
trying to grow with hardship between two stones
just by my window.
Why the seed of this particular tree
choose this spot?
Will it have enough space for roots to grow in free potential?
Maybe it is his destiny
to inspire the answer
about my own destiny and growth
as a wind of Communistic Poland drift my desire for freedom here?
Thank you America for crossing my destiny.

Elizabeth Plater-Zyberk
Miami, FL

I grew under falling bombs on my mother womb — Warsaw — during WWII. Nihilism of the Communism directs me to our "Boogie Street," "Partumiarnia," Warsaw with uncompromised poets, philosophers, artists. I married poet A. Partum and had one son in 1960. We escaped to the USA without money, family, or language in 1969. In Miami I married Seweryn W. Plater-Zyberk, Polish aristocrat, and had three sons. Our first son, Victor, died of cancer at eighteen. Our second son, Anthony (thirty-three), was born with Ondine's curse. Hope plus faith plus love are forming Anthony's power of life. Poetry is my escape to....

A Place to Dream

A place to call home,
To be yourself,
To explore,
To learn,
To have your own opinion,
To have a dream.

But some people deem
They should receive the world for free,
Change what others have fought
And died for.
They want a utopia
That's full of idealized notions
That do not work in the real world.

Nothing is free.
No one will hand you your dreams.
If you put in the effort,
You will get what you want.
Have a dream
And go claim it.

Leah Barr
Creston, IL

The Quality of Life

For every life there is a beginning and an end,
For time within, there is a message to be sent.
Cast the pride of mountains, serenity of streams,
Open your imagination in pursuit of your dreams.
Build a foundation of wisdom, share it with all,
Expose a gracious personality, let it stand tall.
Present a robust smile to everyone you meet,
Give a helping hand to the needy on the street.
Banish hatred and replace with steadfast love,
Uphold peace for all, as on the wings of a dove.
No matter what your assignment, do it with zest,
Never let it finish until you're satisfied it's best.
Grasp power of prayer, let God be your friend,
He will take your hand for pain you may tend.
Nurture your body wisely and train it to endure,
The vast array of challenges that living will refer.
Choose life's work for what interests you most,
Happiness for money is a choice you will toast.
Select a fitting pastime to refresh body and mind,
A necessary relaxation is a treasure you will find.
Embrace your special talents, willingly provide,
A lift to lives of others that are about to subside.
The foregoing is an opportunity available to all,
Cherish the time within as your beckoned call.

Garry O. Hanson
Florence, KY

I am a semi-retired consulting engineer and a US Marine Corps veteran. Writing poetry presents a personal challenge to me and gives me an opportunity to convey to others, hopefully, a sense of enjoyment. During the course of living on the great planet Earth, I believe that everyone confronts thoughts of comparing life's activities and attitudes to where they are versus where they could be. "The Quality of Life" is intended as a possible guideline for this self-examining comparison.

Self-Inflicted

With a heavy heart, my mind is a blur
Many emotions assail my senses as I heard about her
So many questions, but where to start
Others who were closer have suffered more than a broken heart
Young, so full of smiles and laughter
We all seek answers for what comes after
No matter what is uncovered or explained
Life and loss are full of hope and pain
Memories will comfort and surround
But I doubt those who loved her will ever understand
The many questions of why will never quite satisfy
Until the day you see her face clearly amid blue skies
Standing side by side in front of God without fear
Perhaps all answers will once and for all become clear

Sami Korientz
Santa Maria, CA

It Is a Genuine Politic

It is a genuine politic
To whom they epic
Red green republic
Someone else property
Someone else possession
Ice jug
This world is half learned
The verve quest
The queen and the quarry
Americans are flamboyant
Russians are Volga
Englishes are whimsical
French are charming
Italian are Keglevich
Seven red stripe
Six white stripe
With vanilla stars in the
Navy blue sky
I swallow a cube of salt
To defend my edifice
Over his bigotry

Waimar Than
San Francisco, CA

The Parade

Bang the drum slowly, again and again
Bang it in tempo, let emotions reign
Attention, salute, lift our beloved flag high
Salute at attention as its unfurled, sallies by
Those on the sidewalk with somber eye
Watch paralyzed, damaged, injured, lurch by
Wheelchairs, prosthetics, steel braces and such
Seeing Eye dogs, missing limbs, out of touch
Somehow medals, pendants, pins and such
Don't seem to matter, in spirit, that much
Bang the drum loudly, for those who don't hear
Wave the flag wildly for the blind marching near
Segregated platoons, those brave troops
Now come the females, in their own groups
On the sidewalk, the illegals glare,
They are ineligible, so they don't much care
Only, of course, if officials see them there
The noise and the glitz attracted them there
So they brought their kids; they've time to spare
Therefore, in honor of our brave ones, both women and men
Who never again will see, walk, or bend,
Wave the flag gloriously, bang the drum victoriously,
Bang the drum slowly, again and again

Sharon D. Proehl
Henderson, NV

Vol. 1

The Stars and Stripes

Somehow along the way one day,
A plane changed our living way.
We see the falling of thousands of lives,
That crumbled before our very eyes.
And then they raised the stars and stripes
To show the people, they still had life.

There's a lot of lives unaccounted for.
They are not lost, God knows where they are.
He keeps a watch over all.
This is His land, it will not fall.
We look to God to guide us along.
We pledge to the flag, it still waves on.

The battle cry has just begun,
To fight for freedom for everyone.
We are the ones God has called,
I can hear His voice in the wind.
It is written in the sand.
The stars and stripes still stand.

I hear the bugle call.
All the people are marching on,
How they show pride in their eyes.
So forward we must go along,
Giving a hand to help this land.
God bless Old Glory, it waves so high.

Jewel A. Durham
Littlefield, TX

I have been blessed to be born in this great land of America. There are so many things to do to fulfill our lives if we take the opportunity to work at something. I like to paint, make apple-head dolls, and write poetry. I have a great family. I had the pleasure of being a great-great-grandmother in 2015. I was watching television when the second plane hit the Twin Towers. At that moment, I said to my husband, "Well our world has just changed." Then I started writing the "The Stars and Stripes."

Christmas Eve

To prevent the jolly fat man
From turning your
Roof and chimney
Into a dreadful sight
Keep your home fire
Burning warm and bright
Unfortunately he will still awaken
Your bed time slumber
With his hideous ho-ho laughter
That rolls out like thunder
Until he is completely out of sight

Michael C. Schaible
Falls City, NE

I am an author of three books, Eye of the Sleeping Dragon, Time Keepers *and* Quasar. *I like poetry and try to add it to my books whenever I can.*

End Times

Earth's a breaking, hearts a wandering
And a pondering, men hearts fainting
For what is coming upon the earth
Prepare to meet thy God

Heaven's a shaking, earth's a quaking
Tsunami's a coming, Earth's a groaning
Strange things a happening
Prepare to meet thy God

Trumpets a blowing, bright angels a gathering,
Volcanoes erupting, oceans a churning
Read Revelation Yeshua is a coming
Prepare to meet thy God

Third angel's message a going
Over the whole earth,
Messiah is a coming
Prepare to meet thy God

Children of this generation, know your visitation,
Come join this jubilation, take the cup of salvation
You're living in the season of His coming
Prepare to meet thy God

Serious urgent business, no time for playing
Signs of His coming are unfolding
Over the whole world
Prepare to meet thy God

Cynthia P. Grant
Tamarac, FL

Merry Christmas

The Christmas lights were blinding on the streets of old Broadway
Yes, Santa would be coming, we expect him any day.

Streets and sidewalks full of people, hustle bustle everywhere.
Bells were ringing, choirs were singing. Christmastime was in
  the air.

In a cold and darkened corner sits the image of a man
He is old and very dirty, hoping for a helping hand.

By his side a box of pencils, and old orange crate was his seat
"Won't you buy your child a pencil, put some shoes on my
  cold feet?"

There was very little money in a jar that sat nearby
People looked at him disgusted, no kind gesture, no sad feelings,
  not a tear fell from an eye.

It got colder, he grew weaker on the corner of Broadway
Found next morning by a sweeper on the sidewalk where he lay.

Box of pencils, jar of small change, with his almost frozen hand
He had written: "Merry Christmas. Peace on Earth. Goodwill
  to man."

Jo Ann Blunkall
Paonia, CO

Government Issue

A proud American eager to serve
Now disgraced is this what he deserves
Killed sixteen civilians after seeing a horrific sight
Deployed to Afghanistan to face another fight
Not exactly the story this soldier was told
In the military lying never gets too old
Orders were he was to be a recruiter not fight again
The country he fought for lied in last effort to win
He watched as soldier was blown apart
This last act struck him right in the heart
Would this nightmare and insanity ever end
Soldier that was injured was sergeant's best friend
Picked up some liquor to ease an unstable mind
Started shooting innocents his morals now blind
Before the occurrence all agreed Robert was so mild
After military conversion staff sergeant shot a child
Turned into a government assassin then training must be forgot
Return to old life, forget what you saw, forget who you shot
Forget everything in war that you have ever seen
Most important forget training that made you a killing machine

Teresa A. Paul
Henderson, NV

My grandfather said many times, "There would never be another war if our president and other world leaders were the only ones that fought." I agree and I can see how if converted into a killing machine you could lose your heart and your mind. I have the utmost respect and gratitude for every brave soldier in our country. God bless all of you and keep you safe.

Extinct

I feel as if I were a dam about to burst wide open
My emotional outlook on life is bleak
I doubt if I can make it through another day
I can see whether I'm coming or going

My dreams all falling apart before my eyes
I don't know how to act anymore
I feel as if I'm falling into oblivion
I scream for help
No one comes no one hears

I fake being happy when I'm around people
I take long walks and window shop
I try to keep myself busy
But too many things have happened in such a short time that
   made me so miserable

I cry, the beauty that once surrounded me is gone
It all crumbles before my eyes
The buildings whose voices I once heard are quiet, so quiet
My friends all gone
What else is there for me but death

Nelva Concepcion
Bronx, NY

These United States We Love

These United States will show the free world
How freedom's alive throughout this great land.
Our stripes and bright stars forever unfurled:
Heroes we honor with warm pride so grand.

We place trust in Thee with our liberty,
Hold high the lamp as we brave march on.
To absolve all sins, His way to set free
Those loved from our past, bless all who have gone.

View from sunrise shores to shore's setting sun,
High mountains and plains, rivers, love them all.
Farms, cities and towns, united as one:
Blazed in history, pioneers stand tall.

Each day shall we fight, hold strong in our hearts,
Our Constitution, the true way of life.
A culture unchanged, it's glorious parts;
Restore what was lost: families, man and wife.

This Republic stands as none other has
Since all have put forth their fortunes, their souls.
Based on sweat and prayer with a valiant past,
Nation under God, guide *us* toward our goals!

Glenn Voirol
Fort Wayne, IN

American Poet

Age of Innocence

My mommy took me to the zoo
Where I saw chimps and monkeys.
Although they played and made me laugh
I felt somewhat forlorn
Because in that entire zoo
There was no unicorn.

My daddy said he caught a mouse
Because he heard it sneeze.
I thought it was a kitten
Who just happened to like cheese.

I fed it cheese and crackers
So its tummy got quite big.
And even then it craved dessert
Of whipped cream or a fig.

If truly there's a heaven
Where mouses are allowed
I hope my little furry friend
Finds cheese on every cloud.

Paul D. Migliore
Delray Beach, FL

When My Time Comes

I had a dream the other night, it made my blood run cold
A strange voice said, just four short months and you'll be eighty-five years old.

Swiftly I jumped out of bed, I knew not what to do,
That strange voice spoke to me again; it said, I have more advice for you.

No one lives forever. We must leave this world someday,
When you're gone and people talk about you, did you ever wonder what they'll say?

Will they talk about how nice you were, and how they loved you as a friend,
Or will they say you were a wicked man, who lived a life of sin?

Now when my time has run out here, and my race on earth is run,
I hope you'll talk about the good things and not the bad things I have done.

But if I make it up to the pearly gates, I'm sure I'll hear St. Peter yell,
He's from the Seventh Army Lord, he's served his hitch in hell!

Lloyd D. Caskey
Bristol, IN

American Poet

I Pray

I pray to be Thy servant, Lord,
  on the day of recompense,
that then my feet aren't planted
  on each side of the fence.

I pray to not be swayed, oh Lord,
  by those who don't believe,
nor taken in by Apollyon
  whose task is to deceive.

I pray not to be lacking
  when You give Your final test, for
only at Thy coming
  will my soul find any rest.

I enlist to join Thine army
  for the day the trumpets blow,
to inflict the wounds on Satan
  for the pains that we all know.

Glory be to Thee, oh Lord,
  Thy Spirit and Thy Son,
and glory to Thy kingdom
  when the final battle's won!

David Moody
Weatherford, TX

America, the Great

Grandmother took a job to make ends meet
Times were severe, supplies were dear
And there was rarely enough to eat.

She replaced a man who was called to War
To go defend, along with friends
Belgium's cold and embattled shore.

She proudly stood for hours on end
Wielding the torch, she kept on the porch
As she served with the other women.

On the hardest day she grabbed her head:
Two officers emerged, and everyone heard
That Matilda's sons were… dead.

Taking courage from the flags though quite unnerved
Simple pine boxes to rest, she had done her best
To mark their lives and the country they had served.

She hung both flags daily saluting their fate
For she knew that her sons, just babies with guns,
Were two of the "men" to make America, *the great*.

Rhonda S. Galizia
Zelienople, PA

I descend from a long line of patriots. Members of our family have fought in every war. I have in my possession the Symbol of Leslie Faith and Fortitude, a small blue New Testament that was signed by—and attended the service of—each soldier who went to battle. Recognizing that America is at a precipice, like Jeremiah the prophet, I have wept many rivers of tears for my nation, for its survival, for the future of my grandchildren, and, by God's blessing in July, a great-grandchild! God save America!

The Time of Maturity

The time of maturity, it is not
Just our life parts when days became gray,
Vice versa, the sun shines, our hearts are hot
We create, and the Lord hears our pray

In this marked time you are fighting, daring,
Trusting that the future must be grand,
And try always to be thoughtful, caring
For each who is our darling and friend

In these days we gain some special visions
To grasp what's the main in our life's way
With this clear knowing of the omissions
For which we have to completely pay

Just then someone's hands may spark such madness
If it is above all, the soft voice,
And of parting, we sense bitter gladness,
And of love, this difficult rejoice

These years are the time of bitter losses
Which are tearing apart, friend, your heart,
And the prime this unquenchable fondness,
And the fall sorrow so deep and smart

Though the fatigue grows up with each life stage,
We do not despair—our hopes shine
Rushes of youth, the wisdom of old age,
They are with us, and this all—so fine

Leonid Vaysman
Los Angeles, CA

America

Beautiful and flawed: majestic and tilted
Awe-inspiring, random and at times wretched
And for all its flaws, indiscretions
A most glorious and wonderful country
From the Paiutes to the Utes and the Apaches
From the Rocky Mountain to the savannahs—grasslands
Splendid! Spectacular and majestic! A symbol of promise!

The Grand Canyon with its varied hues
To the big horn sheep that roam the plains
To the Hoover Dam, man-made and powerful
Where many were sacrificed for its birth and beauty
To big sky country with its vast acreage of land, cattle,
And mustangs proud, erect and tantalizingly beautiful
To the million lights of Sin City: to the spectacular lights of Broadway

America the inspirer, the conspirator, the motivator, the healer
You whom many emulate and try to duplicate
But with your extensive diversity confuse the world
How you live, how you love, how to be
Innovate and cultivate the diverse cultures of the population
America the great!
My home!

Claudette H. McLennon
Brooklyn, NY

Toxic Toll

I used to love coming here, and not just for the money
My job gave me purpose, my outlook always sunny
Co-workers and management, all with a common goal
Sadly, twenty-five years have now taken their toll
The last thirteen with no increase in pay
"Thank you" or "good job" my boss will never say
Stressful expressions replace smiling faces
Teamwork, trust and support, of these there are no traces
Still I will not despair in this toxic environment
December twenty-second of 2016 I begin my retirement!

Bonna McFadyen
Rockford, IL

Recognition

Long ago
One day in May
When I was young and foolish
I wrote a poem
I was in love with love and spring and you
Now I read those scribbled lines
And to my surprise I realize
I find the words ring true
In spite of my youth I was not a fool,
But perhaps accidentally wise
These are the lines I wrote… I quote…

"Old wintered love they say
Is deeper and richer yet
I'll wish now and then
To be a pauper again,
A barefoot walker
In that one frayed winged
Green-gold noon in May"

There are things that change and things that last
And wisdom passed down from the past
But when I read the words
My eyes blurred
With tears

Laura T. Woolschlager
Wenatchee, WA

He Rides Above the Clouds

(Dedicated to the memory of Chad DeLoy)

He rides above the clouds with no shadow,
Through the peaceful land of eternal sleep,
With all of his fellow bikers in tow.

Always keeping an eye on those below,
May all who have known him no longer weep—
He rides above the clouds with no shadow.

Moving swiftly, forever on the go—
Rising above hills, no matter how steep,
With all of his fellow bikers in tow.

He treasures your friendship more than you know;
May his company you forever keep—
He rides above the clouds with no shadow.

The sun reflects brightly off his window—
Through Lexington, the motorcycles sweep,
With all of his fellow bikers in tow.

He watches you all riding in a row,
Holding your memories of him so deep.
He rides above the clouds with no shadow,
With all of his fellow bikers in tow.

Thomas Koron
Grand Rapids, MI

This is a commemorative poem, which is dedicated to the memory of Chad DeLoy, who passed away very unexpectedly on September 25, 2008. Chad served for many years as a well-respected technician at Man O'War Harley Davidson, which is located in Lexington, KY. He was a very devoted husband, father, son, and brother who was also a very loyal friend to the many people who knew him. There is a memorial motorcycle ride held in Lexington every year as a tribute to his many years of service to his community and to the many lives that he touched throughout his lifetime.

Intangible

I'm traveling down a tunnel but I see no light at the end
In my mind it's there, but then I realize that's just pretend
I can visualize many things, but I'm unable to make them real
I know seeing is believing, but what if I can't feel?
How do you give life to thoughts and dreams? They are things you can't touch
But they are what I desire most in the world so very much
It's the intangible that is priceless and can take our breath away
Or shatter hearts and leave a void until we're old and gray
Hope is a feeling that can help you through sorrow
It will lift you up for a better tomorrow
Material things mean nothing, they come and go
It's your soul that makes you human and makes your life go to and fro

Megan Labarthe
Westlake Village, CA

My Christmas Wish

I wish for peace not in the world
But in *my* family
Life is too short to live with regrets
So love *all* of you... no matter what
I watch the old die too young and the young die too old
Put your differences aside before time just goes...
Imagine...
Growing up without a parent... grandparent... child... grandchild...
Without knowing... *you* are loved!
So wish for love and happiness
Wish for forgiveness... wish for peace
Let all the stars know your wishes...
Remember what it was like to
Just call to say "I love you"...
Dance like no one is watching and smile when someone does
The hugs and giggles...
The monkeys jumping on and in the bed...
Before the mistakes... before the anger
See what is... and what's not... what's true to be...
Feel the love within...
Like I am wishing for the day when I can hold my grandchildren...
Hug my children... watch them make my mother happy with
    a visit...
So while my Christmas wish seems simple in nature... I wish
    it was...
Things that happened so very long ago taking hold of a future
    of unknown...
Wish I may... I wish I might... just hold on tight... to the love that
    still is...
My Christmas wish...

Corinne Soutra
Chicopee, MA

Portly-So

There once was a gentleman of breeding —
A victim of much overfeeding
When his friends called him "portly"
He answered adroitly
'Twas merely his toes were receding!

Edith Murphy
Lynchburg, VA

Christmas Blues

Some fool in Washington gave our jobs away
Now my daddy gets no pay
Even Santa is feeling the crunch
His elves too, he's laid off a bunch
To the North Pole, letters now written
Ask not for toys, please some warm mittens
Just one more gift from you this day
Santa take my mommy's tears away

Mildred J. Siedzik
Clawson, MI

America's Spirit Will Arise!

Awaken O' spirit of America to justice and freedom!
The root of evil has invaded our fruitful land,
Decaying our trees of living waters.
The sting of hatred has blinded you to fall asleep!
My heart cries in despair as a mother in birth pangs
Bringing forth her child into this broken land.
Our forefathers fought for freedom,
To bare our children the hope they dreamed.
For in faith men turned every stone
To make its inhabitants a dwelling place of unity.
Is the global thunder the curse of every man's heart?
Spiritually awaken I saw the hand of God tearing dry soil
As many rested believing they would not die as
Billows of waves rose over the shores where they drifted away
By the sunshine we once enjoyed.
An angel stood before me with a child he saved
Once bound in wheels of metal.
Arise O' spirit of America—it isn't the end.
Awaken by the sound of children's laughter
We held hands till each kin was found.
My heart panted with joy as my spirit praised God
For this generation overcame the destructor
Telling each man His word is true and cannot be broken.
Rise up America to the voices that kept this country
Spiritually awoken setting the captives free,
In the land of the freedom we once knew.

Ipolita Sanchez
Brooklyn, NY

Back and Forth

Having so much alone time it almost kills
But never wanting to go out
Always wanting to get a perfect score
But never having the energy to study
Wanting to go to sleep at 3 p.m.
But my mind keeping me awake till 3 a.m.
Feeling paralyzed in the present
But fearing the future
Wanting to stay in bed all day
But fear what will be missed
Wanting and needing to have everything done
But thinking, "I'll do it tomorrow"
Wanting to make new friends
But terrified of being judged
Going back and forth
Anxiety
Depression

Ashley Weiland
Plymouth, MN

Technology

There they are wearing
  Ugly piercings
   And elaborate tattoos
On smart phones, iPads, and Androids
Eyes focused, thumbs racing across tiny keys
They just talk and talk and talk
Why don't they listen? Why don't they see?

Bro Bob searches a trash can for a bite to eat
Sis Sue lay shivering even though it's 82
Lil' Mae, stands crying on the corner
But they just talk and talk and talk
Why don't they listen? Why don't they see?

Yes, there they are wearing
  Ugly piercings
   And elaborate tattoos

They just cling to their
Smart phones, iPads and Androids,
Eyes focused, thumbs racing across tiny keys
While they just talk and talk and talk
Why don't they listen? Why don't they see?

Constance A. Chapman
Atlanta, GA

Winning Smiles

Winning smiles can go miles
A smile on your face
Works anyplace,
I surmise
Try it on for size
A smile is like a first prize
It is wise and gives you a rise
Any mammy or pappy looks good happy
It is a good ploy
Don't be coy
Bring on the joy
For any girl or boy
It doesn't cost a fee
I like to see
That grin on your chin
Is a real win
It works with any clothing or hair styles
Piles of smiles!

Lauren R. Majcher
Myrtle Beach, SC

2 Cents... of Words and Worth

"In God we trust." The words are few, the coin small, copper...
yet like a one-eyed glass it magnifies America.
O' Motherland! I hear my voice in yours! And see a father in
Lincoln's face. How like a parent, you had drawn
us closer to yourself—when terror hit a place called home.

Rhyme and reason shook their heads: Paris! And now this corner
of the world—California. Hope could have flown! Again!
But stays: its presence a present—ribboned with a bow.

  Father Time stamps his foot (quiet!)
  "Am I my brother's keeper?"

Flora! Fauna! Fur! Feathers! Fin! Shell! All very good
when naked Earth was dressed in gloria. When dust was dust...
when rib called Eve not there; to see, taste, fall.

Tomorrows come. School lessons wait, while children say,
"I pledge allegiance to the flag..."

Christmas morning: outside I toss two pennies
heavenward—for peace on Earth... goodwill to men.
Each found downstairs that week, and what! highlighting where
a washer cleans a swirl of things. As for that other kind?
His help, divine.

A baby
doll in a manger sleeps. I call it Jesus.
Its brow, breast, hands, feet I'd signed—
with kisses from two cents.

And this I heard:
"In you I trust."

Carrie M. Grindley
Oakwood, IL

The Death of My Neighbor's Magnolia

A warm and sunny Wednesday in November.
The last day for the tree, which bravely stood
Remembering its past, if trees remember
Against the blue sky, gold/green leaves, black wood.
The screaming chainsaw echoed through the town
As top to bottom branches hit the street.
It took two days before the tree was down,
Two days before destruction was complete.
The severed sections of the tree lay dead.
The massive creature's life untimely done.
"This was a healthy tree," the workmen said.
More years remained to stand against the sun.
My saddened neighbor, watching, stood aghast
Remembering, like her tree, the years gone past.

Sara Hutchinson
New Castle, DE

My neighbor has had Alzheimer's for many years. Her children arranged for her to stay in her home of sixty years for as long as possible, but they could not take care of her magnolia. It had grown too large for the small backyard, with branches reaching into other yards and leaves covering the property. They arranged for it to be cut down. The morning the tree surgeons arrived, my neighbor stood weeping and protesting, having forgotten that her children had explained to her why this had to happen.

Reincarnation

Reincarnation!
Could it be true?
You were me and I was you!

If I were a god,
I would make it so—
(To be frugal is wise, you know).
All those souls of the human race,
Floating in Heaven, taking up space.

If I were God, I'd have such fun.
The souls, you see, have nowhere to run.
I'd change men to women,
And women to men.
I'd mix black souls with white,
They'd have no reason to fight.

By mixing things up, I'd correct some mistakes.
By sharing DNA, some kindness I'd make.
And if some are angry and don't want to hug,
They better watch out or they'll be a bug!

Roberta G. Starsiak
Dublin, CA

A Lifeguard's Lament

Living near the sea then not
  has made longing my constant companion

I miss seeing the sun's first light
  streaking over dark water to the beach
  like a spotlight on a grand stage

I miss being on a becalmed sea at dawn
  and listening to a silence unmatched by forests

I miss the thunderous echo of stormy seas
  wild and foaming deadly whitecaps
  unpredictable west wind hollow backs
  straining to regain old boundaries

I miss the serenity of patient relentless seas
  weaving endlessly around sturdiest timbers
  weaving, wearing, liquefying

I miss hearing the sensuous hypnotic
  wishing, wishing, wishing sound
  of dying seas in darkness
  as once powerful waves spent at last
  with a final sigh
  surrender to the loving shore

Arnold Marks
Philadelphia, PA

American Poet

The Song of the Dove

Unusual evenings
I have seen
And spent,
With you.

Please, darling,
Come and be
My love,
And listen to
The song of the dove,
With me.

Always shall I
Be yours, as you
Shall always
Be mine.

Please, darling,
Come and be
My love,
And listen to
The song of the dove,
With me.
Come and be,
With me.

Sharon A. Birmingham
Glen Burnie, MD

Fast Friends

Fast friends together, dear friends we will be
Unpretentious, warm, nonjudgmental, brave,
Someone who loves unconditionally…

I am the lock; my best friend holds the key
To open heart, arms, hands, ears — unafraid —
Fast friends together, dear friends we will be…

My dog rewards me reciprocally
Wet tongue licks and tail wags — no mere charade —
Someone who loves unconditionally…

Mother's presence, a source of constancy
Which buoys me against life's buffeting waves
Fast friends together, dear friends we will be…

Her firm hand loosens to a degree
Each time I take lead, each time I behave.
Someone who loves unconditionally…

A dear friend in life — a pleasure is he —
A priceless treasure whose worth won't degrade.
Fast friends together, dear friends we will be —
Someone who loves unconditionally…

Mary A. Gervin
Albany, GA

American Poet

A Sad Farewell to John F. Kennedy

Oh! Why that rendezvous with fate
  In nineteen sixty-three
When death by sniper bullets spent
  The life of Kennedy?
His handsome face beheld a smile
  While riding down that street,
Then suddenly the shots rang out
  And blood ebbed to the seat!
His loyal wife, so touchingly,
  Had held him in her arms
And gazed upon his mortal wound
  In self-controlled alarm!
She kept a constant vigil by
  His silent side in death
Until that sad November day
  When he was laid to rest.
Oh! God! Why must such tragedy
  Prevail upon your land?
Why must a mad'ning, mur'drous act
  Befall a godly man?
A young life snuffed like candlewick
  Seems such a sad'ning sin:
A grieving widow, boy and girl,
  To think what might have been.

Larry Sabiston
Worthington, IN

Beautiful Stone

The day we are born no one tells us we are born to move on
How big is the universe? How many worlds?
But there is only one Heaven
God decides when our journeys end and when paradise begins

I open my eyes; what do I see?
A beautiful world looking back at me
Everything is beautiful in its own way
It comes from the heart
Don't see gravel; if you really look it is beautiful stones
Don't get lost in what money can buy
Spend what you need and share the rest
Know in your heart you have done your best
Invest in God and your love will shine
I can't wait to see the sunset from the other side
My new journey will be a big surprise—when God takes me home

Look to the sky, you will find me in the clouds
You will feel me in the warm air
The thought of me will make you smile
You will know I was there

Marilyn Blackwood
Kalamazoo, MI

On August 20, 1992, Marilyn Blackwood attended a campaign rally for Democratic presidential nominee William Jefferson Clinton in Battle Creek, MI. The day prior was Clinton's birthday, making the rally extra special. After the event she was across the street from the rally site when Clinton appeared to greet with the audience. Clinton made his way down the line of supporters to where Marilyn was standing and reached out to shake her hand. In the excitement of the moment Marilyn extended her arm and grasped his shoulder, startling the secret service agents standing nearby. Surprised, Clinton looked Marilyn in the eyes and asked, "Yes ma'am?" causing her mind to go blank. Grasping for something to say, Marilyn replied, "It's my birthday, too." "Well that deserves a hug," Clinton responded, giving Marilyn a great big hug before continuing down the line of supporters. Nearby someone asked Marilyn if it was really her birthday. "No," replied Marilyn, "but politicians lie, too." Marilyn's birthday was, in fact, August 15th. Close enough!

Don't Pull the Trigger

Land of the free, home of the brave
Welcome?
Not so much anymore, hand guns, assault rifles,
Shotguns, pistols, make us vulnerable to
Look over our shoulder, while going about
Daily life
How can humans deal with the stresses
Of guns in the hands of the mentally ill
People it seems are able to connive
Their way with money or drugs to
Seduce
For money people do stupid stuff,
Ignoring logic for power
Fascination with violent video games
Action movies, killing innocent
Animals for fun
The written word is sometimes
"The best weapon"

Sandra Glassman
Oceanside, NY

The Power of It All

There must be a power of which we are not sure,
A power that has its hand in nature when it is pure.
I am not thinking of cities now polluted,
Nor do I speak of global warming in the news.

I am referring to what an ultimate master
For our original environment once did choose.
The sky in a never self-repeating design
Presents a color spectacle so utmost divine.

Rain, the original production of a natural tear
Like a good cry, soul deep misery does clear.
Wind in nature causes an atmospheric swing
Same like the mind when stimulated does sing.

Water the element we cannot live without
To shape the earth into any formation is allowed.
Moon and sun do not with each other compete;
Theirs is the example how a compromise to meet.

Finally the air must be kept free of disease;
It is meant to put our bodily existence at ease.
It is possible through nature healing of our world to find
Pleasing the elements needs to rank first in your mind.

Alexandra H. Rodrigues
Massapequa, NY

Alexandra H. Rodrigues was born and raised in Berlin during the turmoil of World War II. She worked, danced, and played in Germany, Austria, Sweden, and more. Sponsored as a flight attendant for Pan American World Airways, Alexandra flew the world for nearly twenty years. Later she was assistant to the director of language development where she met talk-show host Barry Farber. He made her coordinator for his language clubs. Alexandra's latest book is Infatuation: Poems of the Heart.

Do Not Dry Your Tears

Do not dry your tears, and look for
The warm sun rays of the forthcoming spring
That will help you soothe in remembering
The golden years of many splendorous things
You had shared with your love of yore,
Life renewed, hopes to share and adore.
Do not dry your tears, but keep your lovely smiles,
You still have a long road of many more miles
For yourself, your friends, those for whom you care.
Tame life by the horns, so just dare
To live on, and once again to fly
In spirit with the love that did not die.

Quoc Sung T. Ducam
Rockville, MD

Quoc Sung Ducam was born in Vietnam in the early thirties. Schooled in Dalat, Vietnam, then in Paris, France, he graduated from high school in the early fifties. After earning a bachelor of technical science from the University of Manchester, England, he returned to France to work as a textile designer and engineer until 1974. Admitted to the United States as a refugee in 1975, he obtained his citizenship in 1983. While at IBM, he earned his MBA from Marymount University in Virginia. Now, retired, Quoc Sung devotes his time to writing, foreign languages, and his passion: photography and music.

What If Someday

What if someday,
The world was released from its burdensome ball and chain,
Brought on by those whose hurting hearts
Surround their lives with pain.

What if someday,
All wars were to cease,
And on every land
Resounded the sweet ring of peace.

What if someday,
All men were pardoned from their sorrow,
And each heart was filled
With the beautiful promises of tomorrow.

What if someday,
Wishes were not as unfathomable as they may seem,
And these ideas would develop
Beyond past an average dream.

What if someday,
Thoughts of happiness and contentedness swirled.
Only on that day,
Will all be right in this world.

Megan Schanzenbach
Ringwood, NJ

I am now sixteen years old and extremely honored to be published by Eber & Wein for a second time. I have now commenced a new and exciting chapter in my poetic skills by participating in Poetry Out Loud, an international poetry recitation contest for high school students such as myself. After winning both the classroom and school competitions, I will be reciting three poems of different styles and genres by great American poets at the Bergen Performing Arts Center in New Jersey. This contest has helped me shape and refine my own craft as a poet.

Patriotic to My Core

The United States of America is the greatest country on earth.
Milwaukee, Wisconsin, is the city and state of my birth.

Veterans put their lives on the line for our freedom every single day.
We're able to make choices based on our own needs, wants, goals
  and when we work or play.

We can express ourselves and our viewpoints with the spoken or
  written word.
We gain knowledge from our life experiences that should be
  passed on and heard.

Creativity is so rewarding and entrepreneurship by inventors is
  alive and well.
It's the land of opportunity to make a better life which should be
  treasured and make our patriotism swell.

Our red, white and blue flag deserves the respect of every one of
  its citizens on American soil.
We're beyond blessed to reside here and with drive, hard work and
  determination, success can result from toil.

Diane M. (Total) Lupker
Beloit, WI

Freedom

Freedoms, do not come granted
Liberties gratitudes, is not a token
Its advantages will never scanted
Our precious rights, left unspoken

Positive attitudes avenues victories
Courage always leads self-confident
Personal decisions brings inquiries
To legacy, silence witness cognizant

At morning, the sun enlighten horizon
Give an example of amplitude power
As ancient days mythology Poseidon
Motivated empire unveil brainpower

The same for generation's procreations
We are the continuance of our destinies
Built upon strong our weak foundation
Choices of everyone, become equities

Joseph Daeges
Omaha, NE

Bold American Freedom

Eagles so graceful and bold
  Soaring high in the sky
Soldiers on the ground fighting
  Praying this day that they won't die

A freedom so righteous
  It was given by blood
Bullets singing whistling Dixie
  While bodies land with a thud

I need a medic
  The phrase most commonly heard
Saving the people who save freedom
  Represented by the bald eagle bird

Wars were waged over and again
  Meanwhile time ticked by
Fifty stars for each state held
  Flags we salute waving so high

It is the American way
  To fight for values so strong
Terrorism could never win
  To America, freedom you belong

Lucas John Guimond
Fort Edward, NY

American Things

The baby lay cuddled in its nest
Its mother whispered, "You just rest"
For one day you'll be a mighty bird
A great bald eagle, of you all have heard
Along with the flag your symbol will be true
When Americans salute their red, white and blue
The Statue of Liberty and the Liberty Bell
Remind us of our freedom won by those in wars of hell
Our United States have great things from shore to shore
Here's a few of those things, but there are many more
Miles of sandy beaches with oceans of stunning blue
Ice capped mountains with peaks of greenery too
Great lakes and fields that stretch across the plains
And wide open farmland with tall sugar canes
Cherry trees like the one that Washington cut down
Plentiful vegetables that grow on the ground
Spaceships and big birds, some feathered, some shiny
Diamonds on a field or in a ring, big or tiny
Musical artists and lots of poets too
Authors with books that are fiction or true
Celebrations of Mardi Gras, Christmas, Valentine's Day
Easter, Thanksgiving and some have parades
Four seasons that give us hot, cold, warm and cool
And even a day called April Fools
As an American I am proud to treasure these things
And the represented freedom each one of these brings

Jill M. Langley
Reidsville, NC

My dad served his country proudly, and to all who did the same, I want to thank you. My mother was a patriot who loved her country as I do. I miss both of them very much and thank them for teaching me America's founding principles. My love for them will live forever.

A Value of Silence

Silence is a bad thing
when the world is filled with fear
and it seems to cover all of you.
Fear makes one antsy
which is a negative pull.

Silence is a good thing
when peace is inside you.
There reigns a feeling
a freedom in your spirit
so you feel whole again.

Whatever is wrong in your world
has been separated from you
and all you feel is peace.
Goodness covers yourself
as you live in the moment.

Tune to what's inside yourself
to what gives you power
to what takes away your pain
and hurt inside the body
so the positive is supreme.

Margaret Rahn
Yankton, SD

Fort Sam Houston National Cemetery

Fort Sam Houston National Cemetery…
Grave markers of veterans honor earth
And also too proclaim vets' death and birth.
Veterans of USA military
Repose with their honor now legendary
And remind us of their noble self-worth.
Grave markers have blossomed but without mirth
In oasis with honor as emissary.
In oasis of honor and dignity
That is crowned with a graced companionship
Dwells a celebratory serenity
Proudly voiced from veterans' heart to lip:
Army, Air Force, Coast Guard, Navy, Marines
Ensured America could pursue its dreams!

Arturo Cantú Hernández
San Antonio, TX

My mother, Mary Cantú Hernández, and my father, Arturo DaviLa Hernández, are both buried at Fort Sam Houston National Cemetery. They were both World War II Army veterans. My uncle, Andrew Palomarez Cantú, who was KIA in Normandy, France, on June 19, 1944, also has a grave marker at Fort Sam Houston National Cemetery. Marine buddy Guadalupe Jacobo and Vietnam buddies, KIA Hilberto Ortega and Durwood Hallam, also have grave markers. Roy P. Benavidez is also memorialized. They, and all veterans, inspired my poem.

Life

Birth comes but once
Death comes but once
And there is life in between
It's this life I hold in esteem

From playground young days
To silver-haired hospital stays

There's the first days of school
Good behavior isn't always the rule

I like to recall moments of joy
And have memories of my favorite toy

There are friends—old and new
Oh yes, there are friends to review

There's the blessing of love
Which comes only from above

Oh yes—birth comes but once
Death comes but once
It's the life that comes in between
Which I hold in so much esteem

Mary Miller
Belvidere, IL

Love's First Kiss

Clouds of dreams from mind's eye.
Silver moonbeams arc the sky.
Angels, each with a spindle of starlight,
like meteor showers, they mist the night.
Across the stage of sky they dance,
finds you at the cusp of solitude and romance!

Debra DeVeney
Ione, CA

When the Cowboy Was King

The cowboy was the first superhero.
His trappings included: a horse, a six-gun, a ten-gallon hat and the
 bravery to use all of them for good.
One man stood above the rest.
His name was John Wayne.
Although some may express admiration for Randolph Scott,
 Robert Taylor, Gary Cooper, or Clint Eastwood.
John Wayne could outdraw them, outride them and win a gal's
 heart like no other man could.
They called him the "Duke," although he was not of noble birth.
He once bought a Santa Claus suit to celebrate the Christmas spirit.
He beat cancer for twenty-five years.
I'm sure the "Duke" is riding in the clouds of Heaven.

Tom Burkacki
Hamtramck, MI

At What Cost

So, ring the bell for freedom
For it's long past due
At what cost freedom,
When freedom wasn't true?

Then ring bell for lives lost,
Loss of limbs…
But also for the loss of *self!*

At what cost!?

When the memories come flooding back,
Of that long ago… *past!*
For the *hopes* and *dreams* that fade
    Fades over time!

Then, when hope arises, again!
Since, it was long past due
For the *soul* that was *lost* and
    Now regained,
From the *carnage,* lain

    So, ring that bell!
And ring it loud and long, for the
One, who gives the *light*
In the midst of that darkness!
To give *peace* and for *hope* to remain

Dorothy Safko
Harrisburg, PA

Ring the praises of (laud) the one who takes us from the darkness and brings us into the light.

I Saved You, You Saved Me

You suddenly appeared from somewhere last February
When my precious Motley who fought so hard fell ill
I wondered whether this was a substitute
In my arms she passed to Heaven of her own free will
You became a great comfort as you persisted
My broken heart was gradually lifted
When you purred, rolled and whirled a pirouette
I laughed again never thinking I could get
To where you saved me and I saved you
No one took you in when it snowed and was so cold
But I did, we healed each other emotionally
Velvety black and white a luxurious sight
Buddy became your name befitting and right
Now you're our buddy who won our love and company
By May you brought your darling wife
Looking much like Motley ready to deliver new life
Where under the tractor she dropped the brood
Of six new friends searching for food
A watchful eye, a mind of your own, freedom loving
You shared the opportunity of your family
On the go visiting neighbors roaming freely
That happens here as long as God provides
Sustenance for all of us, Mitch, Checkers, me, Buddy
You chose to not be too attached, you're welcome
To keep your home with us and keep yourself free to
Move ahead together, I saved you, you saved me

Joan Mays
West Brooklyn, IL

Thank you for including my work. It is a great blessing to be a part of the written word in poetry. The moraine land, root-reaching ravines and Swiss-like slopes of Illinois inspire scenes for writing, music and short stories. There is plenty of room for people and animals to coexist and develop the barrenness so that Constitutional freedoms and rights can be recognized. God gave mankind the earth to preserve and enjoy. New compositions help reading programs.

American Poet

Tears at the Vietnam Wall

The Vietnam Veterans Memorial Wall
in black with many a name,
different from other memorials
of fame,
dressed in white
broad and tall.
After reading name after name
of victims of the war,
I could endure it no more,
looking for something
or someone to blame.

My eyes exploded in tears,
as I cried instantly,
hardly able to see,
recalling of that war,
many fears for our own country.
I cried for the death
of each and every one
who chose to serve,
mocked by those with little nerve,
heroic in life's last breath.

Tony Tripodi
Jacksonville, FL

Abby

There once was a dog whose name was Abby.
She lived eighteen years and that's not shabby.
She was a black poodle with streaks of white.
She loved to jump with all her might.
On bed or couch she soared to the top.
She claimed her spot with one big hop.
Bacon strips were her favorite snack.
She would do a twirl when I opened the sack.
She always growled if I was at home,
Just to tell the guest to leave me alone.
I loved to hold her very tight.
But now it's time to say goodnight.

Blin B. Scatterday
Medina, OH

I taught mathematics for fifty years at all levels during my career. My wife, Suzanne, died in 2011, and I have two children: Dr. Mark Scatterday, conductor of Eastman Wind Ensemble, and Cindy Sabula, counselor of junior high. During my career I served as president of West Akron Kiwanis, as Lt. Governor of Ohio Kiwanis, on the Akron Symphony Board and Education Committee, as president of Summit County Teachers Association, and as president of Ohio Retired Teachers Association. I've received awards: for excellent teaching, ODK, AAUP, OATYC and Kiwanis McChesney Award for Community Service.

My Home

The United States of America
  The long way to say "home."
From the Atlantic to the Pacific,
  Are places I can roam.
From Canada to Mexico,
  Two borders north and south,
And all the states lying in between,
  That's what I'm all about.
My state is called New Mexico,
  My own "Land of Enchantment,"
It's here that I mostly go,
  To further my enhancement.
My town is Albuquerque,
  In the center of the state,
With mountains to the east,
  And volcanoes to the west.
There's a river down the middle,
  This is where my bones will rest.
As you can see I'm proud to be,
  A product of this country,
So here I'll stay and live my life,
  With gusto, and most humbly.

Manny Aranda
Alburquerque, NM

Seeking Freedom

Immigrating people left their homelands of the Old World
in search of a place offering liberty, an inalienable right.
From diverse backgrounds, religious beliefs, and customs,
they demonstrated courage, perseverance and might.

While facing many challenges in North America,
the colonists steadily cleared land for homes and settlements.
As a result, thirteen colonies were established:
the beginnings of state and national governments.

Through a leadership guided by a higher power,
Founding Fathers wrote documents for harmony in the nation.
The Declaration of Independence and the US Constitution
instituted parameters for each social and political station.

Pledging loyalty, hard work, determination, and perseverance,
citizens have proceeded over two hundred fifty years.
Along with many more immigrants seeking independence,
they have continued to seek liberty through blood, toil, and tears.

Through these many years, brave women and men have served
the country based on a set of values shared by all.
Wars have been fought and won to maintain a democracy;
each citizen-soldier knows that there is no greater call.

Yes, God blessed the USA from its colonial beginnings.
From its founding, citizens continue to play an active part.
In a government of the people, by the people, and for the people,
vowing fidelity to our freedom must come from the heart.

Judy E. Russell
Hartford, KY

O Lighten My Load Lord

Weary am I as I look to my maker of a
calm blue sky above. Oh lighten my load Lord —
though plenty is due.

As my strength weakens I humble myself
before you.

Confused, I wept in the long hot sun, tired
covered in sweat. I hear the sounds of war
ring out with cries I will never forget!

My country holds my heart. My flag tucked
away in my shirt. My tears fell hard and tense
with much regret!

Remembering the fields of stone that lie
behind iron gates! I pray no more shall
continue such a fate!

Oh lighten my load Lord that another life
not be taken with these hands you've given.

These hands were meant to love and hold with
understanding! Never meant to kill but to
welcome my fellow man in peace of laying
down our weapons.

Barbara J. Dutcher
Glensfall, NY

I love our country very much — and in writing a poem for the men and women who serve our country, I wanted to try to put myself in their shoes — of how scary putting oneself on the line is and how much they wish all wars would end.

Still in Your Heart

Nothing hurts more than a broken heart,
And when you're sitting there and your world is falling apart,
There's nothing that you can do to put the
Pieces back together again.
As time goes by sometimes on a fly
And when you're faced with your thoughts
And you think to yourself of the what ifs,
And the what nots, of the days and nights,
We spent together.
But it's all over now.
You try to go on with a broken heart and
You try to keep from falling apart,
And when all is said and done you know,
That she's still in your heart.

Lawrence D. Student
Cleveland, OH

My name is Larry Student and writing has been a way of taking my feelings and thoughts and putting them on paper. I am passionate about everything I do in life—from writing, to my photography, to my music, to my skills as a tool and die-maker and master machinist. I've been blest to have a great family and a great group of friends. I love what I do. I enjoy writing about my life. A special thanks goes to a young girl named Kendra. Thank you for understanding me.

A Childhood Memory and Hope

When I was young and just a child
I learned about our nation
I learned the necessary facts
Regarding the independence declaration
I also learned important facts
That caused so much separation
Our country needed leadership
And much cooperation
Of hearts and minds of men of faith
Who worked in cooperation
In Lincoln's keen mind, in his leadership
There was no need for segregation
And so we grew, God blessed our land
We became a prosperous nation
Our land was known as the land of the free
And we exploded in population
Our families had great leadership
Justice ruled in every situation
Until men's greed for wealth and power
Became an abomination
I'm older now and wiser still
I don't sit in condemnation
I pray for the peace God sought and bought
Would rule once more in our nation

Ruth M. Blessing
York, PA

God Bless All Poets

God bless all poets
The ones that like to write
No matter what about
As long as it's in sight

Some are very young
Some on the other side
It matters not the years
Or where they do abide

Some live in the north
Others in the south
Many in America
Some do live without

Some have many children
Others choose to not
Living in America
We can choose the lot

America is number one
The place that I call home
It always takes me back
No matter where I roam

Thank you to our Father
Who takes care of all
And to baby Jesus
Born in a stall

Kayla Kimball
Blue Earth, MN

I started writing poetry when my husband was diagnosed with Alzheimer's disease and I became 24–7 caregiver. Writing poetry kept my mind sharp. I also received much enjoyment and relaxation.

Pop-Pops

Pop-pop. Down they fell
From limbs of a giant of an oak.
Pop-pop. She lifted her face to the clouds,
To the blue that filtered
Through the limbs of the giant.
Then pop-pop, the winds brought them down,
Down, down, popping there on the ground.
"Pop-pops," she declared raising her small hands.
"Pop-pops," she said amazed at the acorns
That rained down all around her.
"Pop-pops." She turned smiling at her discovery.
The wind shifted and breezed a mite stronger,
And acorns rocketed ever downward.
"Ouch!" she cried out. "Pop-pops hit head!"
The oak tree laughed at the two-year-old
Who still continued to gather the acorn caps.
"Pop-pops indeed," tree, wind, and acorns replied.

Catherine Smith
Bumpass, VA

We

We are all brothers and sisters,
no matter where we are from.
Some people don't see eye to eye.
But this USA is not perfect.
It takes a couple people to open
the gate of hell. But love will
turn it around. Most of the
people are true to the red,
white, and blue. And most of
us are proud to live in the USA.
 If it hadn't have been for
the people, who fought for the
freedoms that we have now,
we the people, who are alive,
and here today, we would not
be free, or be Americans, peace
is when people of all colors join
hands, and become one.

Marietta Lillie
Wabasha, MN

And So Shall God Bless the Americas

The Royal Theatre of Drury Lane in London
The Statue of Liberty in New York
Rumors of the next campaign promise and primary elections keep us focused and in touch while the presidential candidates and their families are all out touring the historical trail of dust

Learning lessons in our complex American culture we came close to settling for the day we have only become dreamers
It took searching the nation's rich inheritance to the top of the mountain to hear we've landed and we're leaders together "we the people"

Something to remember is while we were still young we built up strength in our beginnings
As our paths continue crossing passing torches and lighting new ones
In the end I wonder if we're still those suckers for storybook endings

Native American brother your faith in the Great Spirit rewards us a hundredfold like a spell-fire evermore consumed
Native American sister may honored be the name of the wolf singing bellow to your beauty scented by the warm presence of how so everlasting under the moon

Forever shall we behold you in God's grace to commend the hospitality your ancestors have shown
And with that I recite with you now in spirit these endearing words alone:

"And so shall God bless America."
"We're the ole cornerstones."
"We're the great American inaugural."

Ellery Washington
Pensacola, FL

My heart pours out onto these pages with every opportunity to share my works with the readers. As much as they enjoy reading and being inspired, I enjoy making it worth their while and desire nothing more than to ensure they do not regret spending a single penny. I would like to say thank you to our readers, and may you one day enlighten those of us who have inspired you to find your voice.

A Real True Friend

To some she is just an old cat.
To me she is a friend a real true friend.
Especially, when in life people have mistreated me.
She has taught me in last few weeks
what is really important, for she has a health issue.
One doctor didn't want to do any more for her
and said think about putting her to sleep.
But, I went to another that seemed to care
for animals and he helped her.
So, thanks to the second doctor
he gave me more time with her.
Like I said that old cat is teaching me
the real things that matter in life.
For she was by my side when I recently was sick.
Would you be there for your loved ones no matter what.
Trying to do your best to help them.
Like I said, she is a real true friend
and I love that old cat.
Her name, is Hun Bun.

Betty J. Bible
New Oxford, PA

American Poet

Our Flag

I'm so proud of our flag
blowing in the air of the beautiful sky
We salute you in the morning
and best of all Old Glory stands
for us all, but best of all as
a deceased husband was wrapped
in the one thing he loved and still stands
Time waits for no one but
our flag keeps on flying
until it needs a new one to replace
its tired and worn stripes
I will hold it close to my heart forever,
for it represents all who are a true
American and love the flag as my
sailor did

Eleanor Benham
Pensacola, FL

I was born in Gadsden, AL, in 1936. What made me want to write my poem was the desire to express my love for my wonderful husband of fifty-three years. We had four children — two boys in the Army, one daughter who is a nurse, and a daughter who was in the Navy but is now in Heaven. I kept her for forty years before cancer took her away, but I know she rests in a better place.

The Skater

He flies through the ice
with the grace of an artist
at work.
As he glides through the
frozen water, thousands of
diamonds fly through the air.
Only the champion skater knows the
feeling, the freshness, the
beauty of the ice.
Lights flashing, uniform glittering
while he slides across the glistening, smooth
platform.
Challenges to the skater are an everyday
occurrence.
Yes, to be master of his own destiny
and champion to his audience is a fulfillment,
inner excitement — "cannot explain."
To the skater — his world is best!

Ernest Asselin
Richland, WA

God has given me a gift. We all have our own gifts. Thank you to Eber & Wein Publishing. It's not hard for me to get my poetry published; I have one hundred poems and fifty of them were published. Do what you love and it won't be hard!

Survival of the Richest

Oh how the White House blooms
On bloodied dark soil
The dark foundations we have created
On the tattered ruins of wars
The blood still being spilt,
The wars still raging on:
All for the hope of
A better nation—
The best nation

Still uniting to fight,
Still rallying to win
Bombings, shootings,
Brawls for justice
Groundbreaking laws
About people, religion, bodies,
Love
People hurt, killed,
Destroyed

It's survival of the richest,
All on the soil
Of the United States

Rebecca Frey
Red Bluff, CA

America's Fair

The fair! The fair!
   It's come to town
Every year in August
   We look forward to the clowns

When I was growing up
It's all we had to look forward to
Rides, singers, hot dogs and fries
That week really flew

Cows come in from the pastures, horses too
   Hogs, sheep, and rabbits shining new
Waiting for the judges to pick wanting blue
   First or second, if we only knew!

Highest bidders get the best
But now it's all over time to rest
No more laughs or homemade pie
Time to shut it down, say your good-byes

There will always be next year
Already, we can hardly wait
So come one come all, it's great,
To the Logan County Fair the best in the state
So don't be late!

Terrie Amen
Sterling, CO

Cat Beauty Contest

In my putty bonnet
With all the catnip upon it
I'll be the cat's meow in any category

We can write a story
And exclaim poor me
But right now I exclaim meow
In the meow jamboree!
On the avenue, putty cat avenue
I am truly, truly purr-fect company

Marvin D. Goldfarb
Sunnyside, NY

The Tick Tock Raindrops

I was lying in bed one late winter morning
listening to the soft raindrops beat up on my tin roof.
I never had paid any attention before to the way
they sounded, like the tick-tock of an old clock.
Beating time in rhythmic motion,
it sounded like music without a band!
Odd things really occur, if one listens close enough.

Vernon Bogle
Manchester, TN

I am seventy-two years old, and I love challenging crossword puzzles, collecting vintage records and writing.

Who Is There to Speak?

Dr. King is dead
Who else carries the philosophies of truth
Who else will stand up for freedoms denied
From all the people who lied
We think we've come a long way
We haven't even touched the tip of the iceberg today
Who else will fight and follow through
To give the freedoms to the human race
Who else will change the countenance of the human face
There's no one with the same intelligence or grace
That will continue the journey to find its place
Dr. King is dead
Most people are still unsure and unread

Carol Goldberg
Pompano Beach, FL

Snow on the Way

Before we had this upstairs west window
There were only whistles, gong rock, and etched
Contracts with comets. Remember how each
Raced across the sky with no capitals,
Punctuation, or rhyme? One shy star plunged,
Splintered growth and vanished. Nervous solons
Rummaged in the dry reeds until whiz kids
Recast the librettos. Now shall we gauge
What's going on downtown? Looks like there is new
Outbreak of gold fever. Foolscaps amply
Clearer than hand mirrors, too. Rich hour. Oh, here's
Lawrence's notes on mornings! Corn Dance! Pretty
Christmas Eve! Tears! If this world ends, they can't
Say we didn't salvage these wares on our backs.

Jeffery Moser
Aurora, CO

This sonnet conflates the history and development of Western literature, philosophy and religion. Its purpose is to acknowledge our humanity from classical antiquity up to modernity and post-modernity. Poetry was, and always will be, the first genre.

The Marine

My husband was a Marine
   all so few and proud.
He felt like he was under
   a puffy cloud,
so lovely and white.
   It was so bright.
He knew it was a beautiful
   sight.

All dressed in blue, he knew
   what was due.
He loved his country.
   He served to protect,
to keep us all from being in
   debt.
He ran up a hill to save his
   friend Bill.

I'm proud to be an American
   and have the freedom to
do what I can.
   That was my husband the
Marine.

Betty Parry
Pawhuska, OK

My Moat

I had a moat in my yard, I didn't try very hard
For the moat, the moat to get my goat, my goat
All I want in my yard, that's very hard
Is concrete, concrete to make my parking sweet

They say they will be here in a week
With concrete, concrete
To make my parking sweet
In a week

If it's not done in a week
With concrete to make my parking sweet
The moat is still in my yard
And my yard is not hard

I want an alligator, a gator that likes 'maters
Tomaters for my gators
I think gators will be a good guard
For my sloshy, whooshy yard

Filled with a moat
A moat to get my goat,
No concrete, to make my parking sweet
Just gators that eat 'maters

Marcy L. Bowser
Newark, OH

We were in the process of having a garage built, but we had to have a concrete foundation poured first. The contractors had to dig a huge moat-like hole for the foundation; due to weather and other problems that couldn't be helped, the pouring of the foundation kept getting delayed. They say it's better to laugh than cry, so I wrote this poem. Our garage is complete now and looks very nice.

Our Land of Liberty

America, our land of liberty,
God's property.
We have pledged our loyalty
Throughout history.

God's goodness is a reality.
We know the power spiritually.
America is our land of liberty.

We withstood many test.
Praying we will not perish, we
Give our best.

Jewelean Taylor
McKenzie, TN

I have hope in God for America's future. My hope inspired me to write "Our Land of Liberty." Our free democracy makes me happy. It allows us to voice our opinions and make our own decisions.

American Poet

This Blessed Land

Where any person's writings may be published
    without fear of imprisonment
Where masses may communicate freely
    without being labeled dissident
Where everyone has personal dignity
    and the privilege of living in a democracy
Where religious freedom, our Bill of Rights,
    exists for all
Where its people can move freely
    without living behind a wall
Where color or creed is no barrier to success
    and all may strive for inventiveness
Where another man's burden is lifted by love
    through God-given strength from above

Mary Kirnberger
Milwaukee, WI

Myrna's Muffler

Myrna got a muffler, and it was surely due.
Nothing lasts forever, even on a Subaru.
It began with noises loud, raising such a racket.
But the muffler it was not, the trouble was a gasket.

The last time that my Myrna perched high up on that rack,
The Subaru guru Anton said, "Exhaust, rear axle back."
So I then called Midas, as they have the "golden touch,"
Pulling out my ARP card gasping, "It truly costs that much?"

"Indeed it does," says Brian, as he pulled me to the side.
I was numbed by sticker shock as my wallet cried.
"Your Myrna's got a muffler plus, and you know it's true,
Nothing lasts forever, even on a Subaru."

Robert S. Kellogg
Denver, CO

How to Spend a Summer's Day

There's no better way
To spend the day
In the summertime
Than at a ballgame

The vendors will yell,
"I've peanuts to sell,
Ice cold beer, here."
So they claim.

Your friends you'll greet,
When you take your seat.
With new faces around,
Others, just the same.

And so the game begins,
Hope the home team wins,
Putting the other side
To shame.

If you didn't have fun,
After the day is done,
You've only yourself
To blame!

Joyce M. Wilkerson
Clinton, IA

Where Is…

Where is our Elijah…
To sound a prophetic warning in the land?
Where is our David…
Against the giant to take a stand?
Pharaoh rising…
Plagues following close behind.
Where is our Moses…
Our Promised Land to find?
The people grow weary…
Our journey has been long.
Where is our Joshua…
To guide us safely home?

Debra J. Dickson
Bauxite, AR

Morning Star

Morning star light,
So big and bright:
I follow your path
Throughout the
Night. For when the sun
Raises you soon will
Fade. I'll hope to see
You once again, the
Same time as last night
With a grin. And if you pass
Through the sky, you will
Always remain a sparkle
In my eye.

Jeff Varney
Franklin, GA

Gone Away

When I tried to reach you
One a late summer's day,
At your home they told me
That you could not stay.
You have gone so far away
Where I can't reach you anymore,
If you could tell me once again:
"I love you dear, that's all."
Now when I walk alone
And look upon the sky,
My thoughts turn around you
And my question still is: "Why?"
The short time we were together
It was more than I asked,
The love arose between two people
But never, never lasted.

Maria Vanderleek
Inverness, FL

I'm Proud to Be an American

Down the widest main street in USA
I marched with the band on Memorial Day.
Dressed in a black wool uniform that was decorated in gold
To the cemetery we would go.
We stood at attention at Soldiers Square
Honoring veterans buried there.
We played the National Anthem when the flag was raised.
A gun salute was given and taps played.
I love my country.
It has liberty and justice for all.

Julia Hittle
Keizer, OR

I was born and raised on a farm outside Onawa, IA. Onawa is noted as having the widest main street in the USA and the creation of the Eskimo Pie. Lewis and Clark arrived in the area in August of 1804. My ancestors helped settle the area. This poem is reminiscent of my high school days. I married and moved to Oregon in 1955. I have been an Oregonian for sixty-one years. God has been good to me. "Let love and faithfulness never leave you," Proverbs 3.3.

Courage

What makes a man charge up a hill into the
blast of a cannon and imminent death?
What makes a man charge a fortified position
with fixed bayonet?
Is it to prove courage to his comrades?
Is it the overwhelming rush of adrenaline
and the uncertain knowledge of what he does?
Or is it just plain fear that motivated him?

What makes a man charge into a
hail of bullets and artillery?
Is it his pride that motivates him
to prove to his comrades that he is brave?
Is it for God, country and family that he is
trying to save?
Or has his government turned him into a
machine for the road they want to pave?

What makes a man defy all odds to
prove his mettle?
Is it his conscience he is trying
to settle?
Or has his soul become as
black as a kettle?
Or has the Man turned him into
something as vulnerable as a flower petal?

Are all men naïve?
Or do some men just have the courage to believe?

Harry C. Craft III
Wesley Chapel, FL

An Ode to My Nathaniel and Violet Josephine

My heart shakes
Upon the thought of my death
For my soul realizes
I can keep no one…
Tears fall down my face
In understanding
That the cloak that I wear… must be surrendered
For the sake of growth and others' despair…
My children… My darling loves…
For I am dying inside… to keep them forever in time
How my brain hurts!
I'm dying inside
As I bleed these words… that are burned in my mind!
Realization of realities…
I am drowning
In pain… I can't lose them…
No! Not again!
Rebirth!

Phyllis Rose Paton
Perkasie, PA

Unloose, Unload, Enlighten

Knock, knock, who's there!
They do not live here anymore
An abandonment of weight that kept one tossing to and fro
Some burdensome, some grievance, some oppression
Unloose, unload and let them go!
Eliminate all things that're keeping you where you need to grow
A new year, a new beginning
So look at where you were, where are you now and where
You want to go
Freedom of enlightenment, a new beginning, go at your pace
But go forth to where you need to grow
The restraints of knots that tied you down, show it to the door
Impart what has been given to you, make known why you have
This new glow
A glow in the darkness, if keeps going forth will close those
Doors and luminous will light one's path as they go
Don't open the door, allowing those things to return
Allow yourself to be enlightened where you need to grow
  Unloose, unload, let it go!

Odessa Cambric
Los Angeles, CA

Let's Make America Great Again

Let's make America great again
Like the one I used to know
The one I fought so hard for
Through rain, sleet and snow
The one that was once respected
By nations around the world
Which we were first to help
When disasters struck their core
We accepted legal immigrants
Who wanted to come and stay
'Cause they wanted to become Americans
And listen to what we had to say
When at age sixteen
With my respected gun in tow
I roamed the woods freely
Hunting for a buck or doe
When we could speak freely
About any case
Without having to be politically correct
Or be censored and put in place
Let's make America great again
When election is to be
By voting for Donald Trump
Who will again set us free

Samuel Lombardo
Destin, FL

My American Dream

It has always been a dream of
mine to get a job in radio or TV.
I've had unpaid jobs in the business
but haven't gotten my big break.
People have said I'm crazy for
this dream, especially with me
having a disability.
I know I have what it takes.

After saving for years, I make
the big move.
Florida are you ready for me?
Leaving family and friends and laying
it all on the line with everything to
prove.
Murphy's Law has nothing on me
as I'm where I'm meant to be

One step closer to my dream.
I have been told how I'm so brave.
I'm so close to my American dream
I can taste it, reminds me of ice cream.
No more will I live in regret and
be its slave.

Abigail Hucker
Orlando, Fl

The Wind and the Cypresses

Once upon a time, many years ago,
we were young and beautiful,
had expectations beyond hope, then
love and happiness were plentiful.

Leaning our backs against young cypresses,
they promised grow and be very tall,
while we were starting our life's race,
tossing our dreams good and bold.

Winds, passing through the cypress trees,
whispered to us: "Time to go and get it."
We run, toss, jump, the world was ours!
We try hard, and some of us made it.

Today, the cypresses completely grown
send us a sweet and candid rumor saying:
"Give up… slow down… be quiet… silent…
We become old… and, it is time for exciting."

Another generation is following us.
Looking for their piece of triumphs and love,
we had from happiness and love our portion,
and those things aren't any more for us… not for us!

Marina P. Easley Harrington
Glendale, CA

Forgetting Me

You were sleeping when I got there as peaceful as could be.
I didn't want to wake you for fear you wouldn't recognize me.
But as your eyes opened and a sweet smile came upon your face,
You held out your arms to me for a great big embrace.
We sat and talked for an hour or so,
As I watched you slowly go.
Sometimes when you would sit by me with a blank stare on your face.
As dementia quickly takes your life in every single trace.
I know one day when I come to visit I will see
That when you wake up you will have forgotten all about me.
My heart's going to break like never before
And I'll be praying for just a lil bit more.
I'm cherishing this time that God's given to me
Before He takes you home where you'll be happy for eternity.

Frances Reid Morrell
Santa Fe, TX

I Was 7

When does love of country begin?
At birth? No!
It's a growing, learning process—
I believe mine took root, blossomed
and grew on a cold frosty Sunday morning—
December 7, 1941
Having breakfast with family, radio on—
News being on, regular Sunday morning
Until—Pearl Harbor attacked!
What did it mean? *War!*
    I was 7
It meant air raid drills, food and gas ration cards
Young men and women drafted—off to war!
Remember "Rosie the Riveter"? I do!
Mothers, sisters, everyone to work in defense plants
Bond drives, Bob Hope tours, USO on and on
    I was 7
God bless America!
Nowhere in the world do our freedoms abound—
Our America is the best! Wake up all people—
It's born in all people, mine grew and blossomed
    When I was 7

Josephine Ingalls
New Smyrna, FL

Internal Battles

Everyone has a constant battle within themselves. When it comes to making a decision they are torn between the heart, and mind. Which one would you choose. The heart says yes, but the mind says no.

When someone has hurt you and the people you loved, in the past or present, which decision is the right one. Your heart says yes but the mind says no.

Do look at the person knowing what they have done in the past. Deep inside I pray they have learned, and now true to themselves, that they are really trying to come back into the light. Or are still the snakes of evil just coming out to get what they want and then slither back in the darkness. What decision is right when the heart says yes but the mind says no.

These people not caring if they hurt you and everyone around them, they are really trying to help themselves. Just trying to hurt the people around them. Which decision is right when the heart says yes but the mind says no.

How desperate are these people and have they hit rock bottom yet. Do they want to stay in the light and trying to live a good life, or are just pretending to live a good life until they get what they came for. Which decision is right when the heart says yes but the mind no.

Consuelo Giron
Denver, CO

Ruby Beaches

Chris, is a piece of heaven for me
A dose of reality
At times, I speak before I should
Then, I begin to feel just as no good

Space between divides things good, bad or indifferent
Indefinitely, I believe in you, for better or worse
From all coasts
May this be a solemn toast?

I thank my lucky stars for what we have
I treasure this like a pot of gold or secret map
You're a man like no other can be
More precious than any emeralds, sapphires or rubies

Someday my life will end and I'll look back
Into those painted ponies of joined abstracts
Molten burgundy dreams, hot heir of alabaster lettuce
A privilege to be able to love you, I am grateful for us

All I've on earth is time, hourglass sand grains inside
To be able to say I was able to love a man as I knew how
Never could love enough, never wipe his wounded brow?
His heart was gentle to me, never rough or tough stuff
Flying timelessly high, without rules, isn't that enough?

Hope and humility, in hours, knees unite true embrace
For his heart loves me too, remarkably, in all ways
While a Blue Andalusian awaits one lost nephew a ride
Greek fortune for a family no soon plays seek 'n' hide
Indefinitely, I believe in you, never without true food

Natalie Guzik
New Braunfels, TX

My Past

Funny memories from the past,
Can be such a blast,
But ones that are sad
Make us feel, oh so bad.
I laugh at all the fun,
We had in the hot sun.
But playing in the winter cold,
Makes me now, feel so old.
I remember swimming in the creeks,
On those hot summer weeks.
Taking pop bottles to the store,
Now sounds like such a bore.
But buying all that candy,
At the time, felt really dandy.
I wish I could go back to slower times,
And leave all this rush and stress miles behind.

Lois Hite Overbay
Atkins, VA

To Our Congress: You're Americans

Not Democrats, Republicans, Tea Party, left or right,
Jewish, Christian, Mormon, Muslim, atheist
Male or female, conservative, liberal, Independent
You're Americans.

You may be President, Senator, Vice President,
Secretary of State, Speaker of the House,
Speaker of the Senate
Majority, Minority Whip, puffed with importance, but,
You're Americans.

So, be Americans!

Deny special interest groups, sending troops worldwide,
Maintaining unequal taxing, subsidizing agriculture,
Oil exploration, allowing pharmaceutical gouging,
And, never default on salary for military,
Social Security recipients, Medicare coverage,
Remember, you're Americans.
You're one of us!

Denise Hengeli
Plantation, FL

Star-Mangled Manner

It *was* the rocket's red glare,
And the bombs bursting in air.
Now it is the politician's loud blare
And lies filling the air.
The people are angry, hurt and afraid
Of the damage to our country our leaders have made.
We want peace, but not at the cost of liberty,
Which many have fought for and gained our security.
We want all our citizens to have opportunity,
Not at cost to some, but through caring unity.
We want our constitutional rights respected,
Not stolen by a few who feel disaffected.
We want to worship freely in the faith that we choose,
Not be forced to conform or suffer death or abuse.
We want a leader with integrity, honest and true,
Such as Washington, Lincoln, even Reagan too.
We listen to the candidates, fearing the wrong choice,
But the worst thing we can do is not use our voice.
"In God We Trust" is printed on our money,
But too few hearts belong to Him only.
Give unto Caesar what belongs to him,
But God should be first, for He caused the world to spin.
Before any change in our country can begin,
The real change must come from hearts given to Him.
So pray for divine guidance as you to go vote,
But remember, Revelation's predictions might not be so remote.

LaWayne Zemp
Ozawkie, KS

Baltimore 2015

The poet says,
"I am what is around me."
Well, let me tell you, Mr. Poet,
I am not what is around me!
All around me there are rioters
And looters
And arsonists burning down buildings.
They are not me!
They are thugs and criminals.
I am a protester,
Holding up a sign,
Demanding justice,
Peacefully making my voice heard,
Acting within my rights
Under the Constitution.
I deserve respect and protection.
I am not what is around me!

Robert P. Tucker
Lakeland, FL

I am a retired minister and professor of religion, philosophy, ethics and logic. I sat spellbound watching the Baltimore riots following the death of Freddie Gray while in police custody. So much was wrong in that city at that time. Then, amid the flames and chaos, I saw something that was so right—and so American: a woman peacefully exercising her right of free speech, despite the danger to herself. I remembered the words (quoted above) of Wallace Stevens' poem, "Theory." Their irony that day inspired me to write my own poem, "Baltimore 2015."

The MST Bug

Be all that you can be.
Become a regular Army WAC.
But don't get bit by the MST.

The ad was musical and catchy;
The bait a promised GI bill.
Be all that you can be.

And boot camp was my only adventure.
Shout out that I was stylin' and profilin'.
But don't get bit by the MST.

PT and breaking down the weapon,
Loading banana clips — all lessons learned.
Be all that you can be.

Cooks selling joints,
A stellar salad made at KP.
But don't get bit by the MST.

A regular out at the Tiger's Den
Then sleeping it off at the male barracks.
Be all that you can be.
But don't get bit by the MST.

Annette J. Teixeira
Chico, CA

fallen twins

on that tuesday morning
before getting out of bed
the sun was shining brightly
a breeze blew across my head

i poured a cup of coffee
while still in my bathrobe
turning on the morning news
matt and katie seemed so cold

they explained the situation
a jet hit the north tower
the very next thing a second one
appeared to be losing power

being an eyewitness to history
is not something full of glamour
the main problem with it all
for the "good old days" you'll clamor

unfortunately each generation
its own pearl harbor may face
securing lady liberty's promise
is like running an uphill race

Marc Miceli
Nalcrest, FL

The weekend before 9/11 I was visiting my mother in Brooklyn. Saturday we went to the mall to shop and take in a movie. Later we enjoyed the early bird specials at a neighborhood diner. Sunday it was hot dogs at Coney Island. Then we simply sat watching the gulls and boats at Sheepshead Bay. It was late afternoon when I decided to drive home. While on the expressway I looked across the East River. With the sun setting, both towers were glowing like giant gold bars. Regretfully I was unable to capture that unique perspective. This was truly the calm before the storm....

Be Mine

I've been thinking lately what I like
About living in this small town
How I don't have to wait in line
Not at the stop sign not at the gas pump
And not at the grocery store
What I like about this small town
Is that I do have to wait in line for you
For through precious minutes I get
To hear what you are thinking about
So what I'm thinking about is that
In your heart you know that in my heart
I know you are all mine
So when my heart skips a beat
It's because of you
And when you check my pride
I know you love me too
So in this small town you see
I don't mind waiting in line
Be mine

Became my friend
This girl with a zest for life
How she could care
How she could hate
How she always come back
To being great
She left our town
I miss her, her zest for life

Melvin Peter Wenstad
Michigan, ND

Upward Trails

With every leaden step I take
On well trod trails to lofty mountain peak,
I reaffirm my faith in God
And I listen to Him speak…
Soft, mellow murmurs of myriad sounds
Through woodlands dark and deep…
With gentle breezes that abound
On rocky ledges steep…
Such splendid beauty I behold
As I ascend,
Above tree line on mountain highs
My way I carefully wend…
The sun, enhancing expansive mountain views,
Softly as a blissful sigh…
With billowing clouds and faultless
Panoramic hues,
A spiritual union of earth and sky,
And once achieved these alpine heights,
At no little energy expense…
There is no more loudly heard…
Such awesome reverence!

Josephine Tambo
Chelmsford, MA

I am eighty-three years old and a retired speech pathologist. I have worked with speech- and language-impaired children and adults. Though I was born in New York, I worked and lived in different parts of our beautiful country. When I was younger and more active I enjoyed the outdoors and nature. Hiking, climbing, and skiing — in the Rocky Mountains as well as our White Mountains — I have enjoyed so much natural beauty available to us with a little effort. My poem "Upward Trails" is but one of several I have written about beautiful climbing/skiing vistas, which to me always seemed reverential. I can only hope that my "word painting" conveys some of that beauty!

Earthly Life

Listen to the voices of the wind
Whispers on the breezes, murmurs in the calm
And know they speak truths and lies

To see the world the way it is
To know you live in chains

The only true freedom offered you
Before you still remains

To serve kings of wealth and power
In this earthly place

Or the mightiest King of the heavens
Who is eternal power, mercy, love, and grace

Dark and fearful storm clouds gather
O'er the horizon just ahead

A day of kings approaches
To fill the unsaved heart with dread

Only One might save you
Hold to Him with all your might

He is your only hope for freedom
From the chains of this earthly life

He is our true king and savior
His name is Jesus Christ

To find Him is not difficult to do
When you draw nearer to Him
He will draw nearer to you

Roger L. Willey
Silverton, OR

I Am America

You've come so far great lady in so short a time
A leader among nations, appointed by the divine
You've known wars, depressions, struggles and strife
Your sons and daughters have willingly given their life

America, America how bright your promise still
Many hopes and dreams are longing to be fulfilled
The land of opportunity sings her siren song
Those who yearn for better times are singing right along

My people come from far and wide, we are diverse this land
United in the red, white and blue, on her we take our stand
We grouse about our politicians, complain about the weather
But should our shores be attacked see how we pull together

America, America long may your freedoms flow
Gently o'er the land may the winds of prosperity blow
Let the voices of my people sing forth their mighty song
We are America, to this great land we proudly belong

Nancy J. Medlin
Chesapeake, VA

I'm a widow. I have three grown daughters and three almost grown grandchildren. I live with my oldest daughter and her husband in Chesapeake, VA, about forty minutes from Virginia Beach. I became a born-again Christian in 1975 and shortly after that began writing poetry. Jotting down thoughts in rhyme, the words come easily to me. I rarely have to labor over a poem. I feel it's an inspiration from God. America has been in my heart for the last few years and I've written my thoughts in poetry. This is one of them.

You Gave It All Away

smothered by the thoughts of you
and all the stuff you put me through
can't believe I let you do
this to me
never weak but always blinding
the string of lies I'm always finding
about you

I gave it all away
and for this I had to pay
you never seemed to care
but for you I was always there
now if you could only see
how good he is to me
no regrets for leaving you
something that I had to do

haunted by the image of you
and everything we used to do
I never saw that side of you
before
never scared and always fighting
the pain inside is slowly dying
from me

Cyndi S. Anderson
Rockwell, IA

Leave Your Love with Me

Leave your love with me
I'll hold you hands forever
Leave your love with me
No more tears in your eyes
Leave your love with me
I'm walking in the summer stars
Leave your love with me
As the night fall I'm waiting to hear
Some music from the 1930s
Leave your love with me

Jack Camp
Boston, MA

Sounds of Nothing

I am one with the silence,
the rush of the hush:
the numbness of quiet, the
absence of din.
The music of life, sweet breath
of your words
no longer hold spellbound my ear,
and I shall hear not your voice lilting clear
'till you say that you love me — again.

Jerry Staudenraus
Moses Lake, WA

Proud to Call You Daughter

The waiting is over
  The family is stronger
Yes we're so lucky now
  So glad you chose us
We have been missing you badly
  With open arms we welcome you gladly
We are proud to call you daughter
  So glad you love our son,
Our love for you is deeper than ocean waters
What an honor you bestowed us
  The family has gained a pearl
You're the crown to our royal furl
  One thing to be sure of
This is a perfect forever
If not forever we shall perish together
We are proud to call you daughter
  So glad you love our son
Our love for you is deeper than ocean water
  This is true too our hearts you've won

James Edward Horton
Sutherlin, OR

I Love the USA

America is my home, sweet home;
None other is the same.
I love the good, old USA;
There is no sweeter name.

I am free to live my life,
Wherever I might choose —
As long as I am living right
And following all the rules.

It is not the nation I once knew;
A lot of things have changed.
No, it is not perfect;
Some things I'd like to change.

I'd like to see more peace and love
And all hate disappear
Between the people of this nation
And people everywhere.

Let's stop all wars, lay weapons down,
Just for a little while.
Just try to love our fellow man
And just give peace a trial.

Sarah Tuttle
Wellington, OH

Crossroads to Liberty

We hold our breath as we listen to the political speeches.
We only hope everyone checks out all the contenders.
Americans should know we cannot make the same error.
Electing a leader is serious.
The success of the nation depends on this.
Now we must unite to take back our country.
God bless America.

Dianne Mombaur
Lakewood, NJ

Essence of Milford

Connecticut is a treasure trove!
For those who are new to the state
Or folks lucky to have visited here
A spectrum in the realm of exploration
From miles of beaches to various lighthouses
Come at certain times and you become empowered with ever-changing moods
Or physical changes in atmosphere
Many will appear really just breathtaking
Go hiking, and see how much wildlife you encounter
Allow these areas to encompass you figuratively
Essence of an artist's dream

Greg P. Renner
Milford, CT

Indian's Canyon

There are Indians in the canyon,
Surviving for hundreds of years.
They pay the price of seclusion,
With blood, sweat, and tears.

Ride forty miles to find them,
Through rocks and waterfalls.
Unravel their life of mystery
Carved in the canyon walls.

Don't despair the discomfort.
Learn the Indians' ways.
Trust the eyes of kindness.
Experience the older days.

Buy the trinkets for sale.
It's all the Indians own.
You will cherish the memory
Upon returning home.

Mark Franko
Hutchinson, KS

Your Story

through my efforts I have forged
a new career at my own company
when I failed out of college

through my self reflection I created
a new life following my own passion
when I lived amongst roaches

through my constant vigilance I broke free
of the voices everyone expected of us
as I discovered my true self

through my isolation I taught myself
how to love everyone for who they are
as I learned how to love myself

through my own discipline I carved
a path to new love, living, and peace

through my resolve I learned
how to embrace darkness and death
as my friends chose ways out

through my willpower I rewrote
my own story at twenty-two years old
that's my story, how will yours be told?

Kenyan D. Burnham
Lubbock, TX

Red

Red should be her name
Classy lady who deserves some fame
Working hard to get things done
Too much to do; always on the run
Go out and dance and have some fun
You'll be the life of the party number one
A regal, loyal trusting friend
I am here for you until the end

Mary Ann Caruso
Laurel, MD

Honeysuckle Days

I long for the days of spring
Those long, sweet honeysuckle days
When the violets bloom with their sweet perfume
I want to watch the birds return
The winter is dreary and cold
To listen to frogs croak,
Hear the buzz of a bumblebee…
Would be a balm for me
Hasten oh spring
The winter is long
I am ready for your song

Marilyn Shavender
Virginia Beach, VA

A Veteran

I met my friend on a hardwood bench
On a very cold October day
His hair was long in need of a cut
And his beard of many a day
I sat down and said hello
He turned and his voice was low
I'm Jim, he replied, with a tear in his eye
I felt like I wanted to cry
No socks on his feet
And his shoes were beat
I felt sorry for this man of old
Our friendship was born
On that cold October morn
Two people on a hardwood bench
Jim was a veteran of World War Two
He never talked about that war
It was more then he could do
Then one day, Jim passed away
Now I go to that bench almost every day
And think of my friend of old
What he went through for me and you
A veteran of World War Two

Gloria R. Smith
Lyons Falls, NY

God bless all veterans.

Vote for Trump

I'm very angry
  I feel the pain at the pump
That's why my vote
  Goes to Donald Trump

You can go on a Cruz
  You can even Rubio
You can join John
  But, that won't make it go

In 2016, my friends
  It's time for your vote
Don't take it lightly
  It's time to take note

It's time to get it on
  Get up off your rump
Go and cast your vote
  For the man, Donald Trump

Bob Bradstreet
West Covina, CA

I'm eighty-three and happily retired from forty years of banking and ten years of security. Married forty-six years to Berit, we have two sons and two daughters. I've been writing poems since 1965 and have studied in poem groups and at UCLA. I created a lyric in 1970, with music by Solomon Burke and recorded by Ray Charles. I was reserve Deputy Sheriff 1983–1993, volunteered in police work for twenty years, was president of Century City Rotary, volunteered over fifty years in total and worked for fifty-five years.

The Little Girl with the Grain Bag Dress

In the middle of the 1940s, everyone for girls
If you didn't have a dress made from a grain bag you were not in style
The little girl with the grain bag dress
Sometimes you might find someone with curtains, the same as your dress
Or someone have a dress in school with the same design
The little girl with the grain bag dress
Some people made sheets out of grain bags
They were not the best to sleep in, kind of rough
The little girl with the grain bag dress
The grain bag had a real pretty design
My mother used to wash the bags before she used them
They only lasted, the design, for a few washes
Some people cut up the dress after the color is gone to use them for dish wipers
My mother had several patterns to make different dresses
The little girl with the grain bag dress
The colored bags only came in chicken or cow feed
I am the little girl who wore those dresses made of the grain bags
The little girl with the grain bag dress

Maxine Dickinson
Smithfield, ME

That Special Day

All heads look upward
Into blackness
We stare
Feeling the excitement
That all of us
Share

The orchestra's playing
And the fireworks scream
They
Climb higher and higher
Then they careen
Gigantic bursts that
Sparkle and gleam
Fall to the earth in
Glittery streams

The reflections are mirrored
In all of the eyes
We scream in our
Wonder
Caught by surprise

In case you are wondering
It's like
Mom's apple pie
Happy birthday America
The 4th of July

Charlotte Neukam
Redondo Beach, CA

This invitation to submit a poem was received on March 1st, my seventy-first birthday. I could not have been more pleased. Thank you! This was written to be read at my writing class for the upcoming Fourth of July, a few years back. My hope is that you see what I saw when writing it.

Forever Freedom

In this beautiful country we live in
we all are born free.
This land that we live in is equal to
all of us.
We fight among ourselves and as far as
I know we are all descendants off different countries.
But even the blood is the same color.
We can call ourselves true Americans because
if you are born in this country, we are
mixed blood.
Most people don't think of that.
The best part of this every time there
is a war people come here to have peace.
Yes, another American is born.
So, let's just bring thoughts together
And be thankful we are *free*.
Yes, I am proud to be an American,
and would like to keep America this way.
So God bless us and keep the country
we live in this way.
Oh, yes we live in America *the land of*
the free and the brave

Neva Rootes
Largo, FL

Our Founding Fathers

Through our history we have slaved
and paved the way to make a better day.
We have bared our souls for a quill, and given
our last dime to set sail, learned lessons to
bend wills.
   Through the weave of eyes we disguise our
distant futures with hopes in solid alibis.
So I bring forth my armies and angels
to descend. This is the age of innocence, the
day of enlightenment, the only reason why
this should make any sense.
   So we move away from the hellos and
goodbyes. We move away from blame and
deny. It's our move and we're charging
our fires to blaze the open night and
seize the skies!
   Our words are worth more than the pen to
the ink. We must challenge our love and
strength, and push it to the brink. We
must learn betterment of one's self, in
contrast to instant convenience, or we'll be
extinct. We must be triumphant and glorious is the
leaders we name. We must be wise and semi traditional
for the leader's way. And steadfast and reliant
on what the leader shall claim.

Sarah Beth Tomkins
Broomfield, CO

To the leaders we've followed and the wills we've bent: we grow from these men. Thank you.

The Soldier I Never Knew

Being so close to death in the field
taught him how to live life, but for a Green
Beret a civilian world only caused him strife.

He stood against the enemy,
even when no one else would,
and held on to hope as long as he could.

A forgotten name on a paper
is all he thought he would be,
but his Fire Team would soon make him see.

Forever he is gone but his legacy remains.
He was a soldier that gave all
and asked for no gain.

So when the C-130 back hatch opens
and the wind rushes in, you will hear him say:
Troops! It's time to be men.

Samantha Hall
Seminary, MS

American Poet

Until There Was You

Until there was you
I never knew I could be this happy

Until there was you
I never imagined two hearts could share something
Something so deep and beautiful

Until there was you
I never believed one person could change my world
In so many amazing ways

Until there was you
I never knew I had a living purpose

Until there was you
I never knew true love
Until I fell in love with you

Anthony Ruiz
Manteca, CA

Proud Allegiance

You lift up your eyes
To the stars and stripes
Blowing softly in the breeze
It's the US flag—an emotional sight!

It says respect, honor and peace
It will fill your heart and mind,
Remembering happy victories
And children pledging rhymes!

It is a symbol of our nation
Draws attention everywhere
And proudly it will always wave
The spirit of glory, a love declared!

So proudly we salute
The US flag forever!
United we will stand
All Americans together!

June A. Larson
Waukesha, WI

Clouds

Clouds… beautiful, ominous, powerful, soft, fluffy,
Mammatus, buttermilk sky
Blue shining through, "sucker holes"
Black, threatening with streaks of
Lightning-ground strokes, cloud-to-cloud
Rain shafts,
Some heavy, some with light shining through.
Thunderheads, anvils, wall clouds,
"Twisty tails" hanging down —
Each sends a message of hope or destruction.
Welcome rain — torrents or showers, fierce or gentle,
Turning windmills to pump water to thirsty cows
Turning wind turbines to power cities
Clouds…

Jo Nelle Graber
Albuquerque, NM

Our Freedom

American freedom—different from other countries? You bet!

So much freedom that it is a big responsibility to handle it with
respect and appreciation! Born in America—live and die in
America. One nation under God,
with liberty and justice for all!

So much we owe to our forefathers—building this nation, trudging
in the snow to the first Congress,
with great courage and love for country. A great mission that
would remain in the minds and hearts of the people forever.

God-fearing forefathers.

And today we go our ways—it's somewhere in the back of our
minds. Is the
Pledge of Allegiance still recited in the schools? "I pledge
allegiance to the flag of the United States of America." And then in
third grade we sang: "It's a grand old flag, it's a high flying flag"—

I still remember the words today, and I smile.

Let's stop and think—stop and pray—for all the freedoms we still
have today—and be ever so grateful. What can we do to support
our country? Celebrate our rights? Support our government
and military?
Think about it. Make your own list.
Put at least one of them into action!

Let's honor the courage and the love of our forefathers
because that love can still light the America of today!

Shirley A. Westbury
Richmond, VA

I write "poetry." It's so very heart-warming to have a "witness" to thoughts and feelings and to share with others and read their poetry. Retired, I am—as Yoda would say!—and loving it. I have ten nephews total: four newphews, four greats, and two great-greats. Thanks to Eber & Wein Publishing for this great opportunity to write about my country. Let freedom ring!

Heartbreak

It is the perpetual mental state
where unwavering sorrow rules
and the bloody silence keeps its borders

It is prison's firm religious walls
without locks or padlocks
where a conviction is purged
death in life
metastasis of blindness and cowardice

It is diabolical spell
ancient burden of earlier faults
that with grief she drags my soul

It is absence, infinite space
where body and soul wander
stunned in an absolute devastation of words

It is human inability to revive the love
whose distant silhouette
it inevitably fades
between the utopia of the future
and the mists of the past

Jorge A. Duarte
Derby, CT

My Love

My love goes way back in time to beautiful happy days
When we were young and full of hope and love was on the way
We struggled through the following years
We worked and loved and prayed
Our love grew stronger through the years
And increased day by day
Soon we were alone again and we grew closer still
We seemed to be one person
With one heart, one mind
One body, one will
And then you left me
The Lord called you home
And I was left here by myself
And I was all alone
I felt like half of me was gone
And I will never be complete
Until I'm called to Heaven with you
And kneel at our Lord's feet
Amen

Ruth E. Schowalter
Santee, CA

First I would like to thank our Lord for leading me all my life and giving me this chance. I was born into poverty, the second oldest of ten children. I had to help my mother raise my brothers and sisters, so I was unable to graduate from high school. I have worked hard all my life, but only in America — with hard work and perseverance — could I have achieved what I have. God bless, America!

Time

Enjoy your day as it comes
with joy and appreciation
from sunlight to dawn
from each minute to hour

Embrace as it is your last
with no regrets for better or worst
cherish each precious moment
with each glory day that God brings you
with your counting blessing
as a gift

Time is the essence
with each hour that we breathe
with each memory we form
with each celebration we create
with each step that we take
with each legacy we build
until we reach to our endless day

Live life to your fullest
and make the best out of it
to show a good example to all
karma is the seed that you sow
like a flower that you plant
comes in beauty or bad
from day one of your birth
to the final day of your absence

So seek kind to other
for the reward that you make
for the given return
from your graciousness like

Hanh N. Chau
San Jose, CA

Two to Love

As I stand alone, my tears are falling freely
Sadness appeared on my face with despair
Feeling like the world ends
Not realizing what's troubling my soul
Feeling emotional for what my heart see
As loving one man, but to a distance with a heavy heart
My eyes see another man, a stronger heart
This is more than a love, it feels like a breeze of an open heart

Dorothy Ann McFarlane
Maynard, MA

Election Day

Election Day is the time to vote. For months we
have listened, and listened, to the candidates tell us what
They will, or not, do if elected.
The time to vote, the choice is up to you, God gave
you a brain to use, use it wisely. Think hard before
you vote. Check them out, are they honest, or just a lot
of talk? Remember you have to live with them until
next election, by then the damage can be done.
The election by God of certain people for salvation
and eternal life, is the only one you can trust.
So when you vote, vote wisely for eternal life.

Darlene D. Stoermer
Greenville, IA

American Poet

The Freedom of Me

I'm trapped in a bubble
Where I'm anything but me
I look out from the trouble
This is what I see
Kids being themselves and chatting with friends
I wonder if this is really the end
I scream for help so very loud
I want to be me, I want to be proud
Not some random girl who wants to fit in
I've got to be me and in my own skin
I have to get out
To be finally free
I believe, I am no longer stuck
I am now me

Sofia Masciale-Walmer
Washington Boro, PA

Hand in Hand

The world is an evil place,
That much we can agree.
But when we're walking hand in hand
My world seems to be free.

The world isn't an empty space,
No nook or cranny deserted.
But when we're walking hand in hand
My beliefs are converted.

The world is a lonely place,
Hearts are easily bruised.
But when we're walking hand in hand
Mine will never be misused.

The world is a beautiful place,
Full of love and full of wonder.
Because we're walking hand in hand
My world will be stronger.

Rebekah Yoder
Lynchburg, VA

Everything Changes

Tired of hiding behind a disguise
Chained in place
Left my heart behind
I'm ready to resign
Change the pace
Dispose of all the lies
It's not about someone
The story goes as it was written
Say good bye to innocence
Like turning the page, in a sense
Picking up something that has been bitten
Caring for what was left behind
The kaleidoscope spins, turns, changes
Adaptation is key
There is no more room left for dodging
In growth there are many stages
Life is full of different ways,
Nothing ever remains the same

Mariah Greatorex
Winslow, ME

Come to America

I came across the ocean
From a country across the sea,
To a land flowing with milk and honey
And all was so new to me!

I came with my young parents
From a land of killings and war
To a country where we'd be free
And life is never a bore!

Here my dad has found a job.
We're not hungry anymore.
We enjoy the peace and quiet
And are grateful to be free of war.

I go to a free school every day.
I have learned to read and write.
My clothes come from a Goodwill store
But I'm free to play and pray as I like.

Yes, we've come to America.
We are grateful they have let us in.
We thank God for this great country.
May He bless it again and again!

Molly Randall
Camden, SC

Index of Poets

A

Aiken, Lois M. 46
Aker, Janie 159
Amburgey, Patricia A. 138
Amend, Ariel 144
Amen, Terrie 267
Anderson, Cyndi S. 301
Anderson, Rose Dyess 82
Aranda, Manny 254
Arrigo, Nicolette R. 15
Asselin, Ernest 265
Atzert, Eleanor Pearl 174
Aul, Loretta 154

B

Bailey, Lonnie 126
Bangert, Gordon 182
Barnes, E. H. 116
Barr, Leah 202
Bass, G. L. 65
Beavers, Annunziata 170
Belensky, Marie E. 40
Belokosa, Bozana 160
Benham, Eleanor 264
Bible, Betty J. 263
Biraben, Jo 53
Birmingham, Sharon A. 234
Blackwood, Marilyn 237
Blagrove, Pauline E. 112
Blakeny, Eleanor Shannon Lee 111
Blessing, Ruth M. 258
Blunkall, Jo Ann 210
Blystone, Catherine J. 19
Boal, B. J. 184
Boggs Cordova, Jó Ann 32
Bogle, Vernon 268
Bowser, Marcy L. 272
Bradstreet, Bob 310
Brainin, Emil 109

Braley, Oleta P. 39
Brannick, John 47
Brinston, Jacklin P. 69
Brock, Robert E. 135
Brown, Daryl D. 95
Brown, James B. 60
Burkacki, Tom 249
Burnham, Kenyan D. 307

C

Cambric, Odessa 283
Campbell, Charles Andrew 99
Camp, Frances Elaine 34
Camp, Jack 302
Caputo, Evelyn 21
Carberry, Marshelle 38
Carden, Rhonda R. 165
Carstens, Patricia L. 104
Caruso, Mary Ann 308
Caskey, Lloyd D. 215
Castaneda, Jesse 80
Cato, Fred, Jr. 168
Chapman, Constance A. 228
Chau, Hanh N. 322
Compo-Pratt, Paula 176
Concepcion, Nelva 212
Conrique, Samantha 137
Craft, Harry C., III 281
Craft, Jacqueline 139
Crawford, Diane 28
Culling, Jeff 68

D

Daeges, Joseph 243
Deal, Mary 146
Deckard, Janet Sue 73
DeFrier, Anne 179
DeVeney, Debra 249

Dickinson, Maxine 311
Dickson, Debra J. 277
Dobitz, Roger H. 118
Drebes, Roberta E. 187
Duarte, Jorge A. 320
Ducam, Quoc Sung T. 240
Dunham, Elva 140
Durham, Jewel A. 207
Dutcher, Barbara J. 256

E

Easley Harrington, Marina P. 286
Ehlers, Darryl 67
Elkins, Alfred 63
Etheridge, Diana C. 98
Evan, Pat 74
Evans, Kayla 78

F

Fairfield, Dorothy B. 163
Fisher, Clata 87
Flower, Katherine O. 183
Floyd, Dea 194
Foote, Lloyd S. 89
Forshee, Ann Marie (Sandy) 198
Franko, Mark 306
Fredericks, Daisyann B. 41
Freemyer, Linda M. 70
Frey, Rebecca 266

G

Galizia, Rhonda S. 217
Gallant, Ann 35
Gamache, Therese Jacques 29
Gayden, Malik 42
Gervin, Mary A. 235
Giron, Consuelo 289
Glassman, Sandra 238
Glessner, Tyrone 64
Gloff, Gretchen L. 103
Goldberg, Carol 269

Goldfarb, Marvin D. 268
Goodlow, Antoinette 133
Gordon, Gene 157
Graber, Jo Nelle 318
Grant, Cynthia P. 209
Greatorex, Mariah 326
Grindley, Carrie M. 230
Guimond, Lucas John 244
Guiney, Mable M. 96
Guzik, Natalie 290

H

Ha, Andrew K. 37
Hager, Bobbi Jo 24
Halley, Lois 131
Hall, Paul 83
Hall, Samantha 315
Hanson, Garry O. 203
Hanze, Hilda 27
Hart, Stephen David 113
Harwood, James 152
Hengeli, Denise 292
Henkels, Michelle L. 121
Hernández, Arturo Cantú 247
Hill, Dianne 26
Hittle, Julia 280
Holt, Connie R. 7
Horton, James Edward 303
Hucker, Abigail 285
Hunt, Joan 86
Hurley, Carolyn 169
Hutchinson, Sara 231

I

Ingalls, Josephine 288
Irwin, William D. 48
Italiano, Antoinette 170

J

Jen, Alyx 147
Johns, Melissa 90

Johnson, Colleen S. 119
Johnson, Krisann 155
Jones, Artist Clay 136
Jordan, Anthony E. 123

K

Kairys, Aldona 84
Kaufman, Carol 193
Kellogg, Robert S. 275
KenKnight, Jane P. 12
Kimball, Kayla 259
King, Steve Arlington 33
Kint, Mi Mi Sandy A. 20
Kirnberger, Mary 274
Kisler, Sandra 57
Knight, Alan 100
Korientz, Sami 204
Koron, Thomas 222
Kutzer, Dolores 66

L

Labarthe, Megan 223
Lane, Malcolm 143
Lanese, Peggy 200
Langley, Jill M. 245
Lani, Althea 75
Larson, June A. 317
Lassiter, Virginia Gail 44
Lillie, Marietta 261
Logan, Gail 195
Lombardo, Samuel 284
London, L. J. 93
Love, Marilyn 43
Lupker, Diane M. 242

M

Majcher, Lauren R. 229
Manning, Lisa G. 150
Marks, Arnold 233
Martinez, Daphne 13
Martinez, Joann C. 106

Martin, Philip N. 56
Masciale-Walmer, Sofia 324
Mateya, Charles F. 130
Mays, Joan 251
McFadyen, Bonna 220
McFarlane, Dorothy Ann 323
McGee, Jasper 76
McGinnis, Debbie J. 54
McGraw, Rosemary 167
McLaughlin, Maureen 132
McLennon, Claudette H. 219
Medlin, Nancy J. 300
Melvin, Lawrence 61
Mendez, Yolanda Orozco 97
Meyer, Janice R. 128
Miceli, Marc 296
Michanczyk, Michael J., III 91
Migliore, Paul D. 214
Miller, Carol A. 59
Miller, Mary 248
Mohl, Allan 79
Mombaur, Dianne 305
Monroe, Brenda A. 88
Moody, David 216
Morrell, Frances Reid 287
Morrow, Milton 10
Moser, Jeffery 270
Mulcahy, Dianne 93
Murdaugh, Cleatus C. L. 49
Murphy, Edith 225

N

Neukam, Charlotte 312
Nguyen, Minh-Vien 114
Nouel, Nieves T. 190

O

Obeng, Raymond 142
Ogman, Beverly 58
Oswald, Nancy L. 102
Overbay, Lois Hite 291

P

Parry, Betty 271
Paton, Phyllis Rose 282
Patterson, Betty R. 14
Patterson, Patrick L. 188
Paul, Teresa A. 211
Perlinger, Donald B. 105
Petrizzo, Ann Marie 172
Phengphong, Xaysouvanh 141
Phillips, Helon 101
Plater-Zyberk, Elizabeth 201
Pratt, Amy 6
Proehl, Sharon D. 206

R

Rahn, Margaret 246
Randall, Joy Dockery 158
Randall, Molly 327
Ransom, Donald 110
Rausin, Michael 17
Ray, Sally B. 151
Renner, Greg P. 305
Richard, Anna 175
Richmond, Florence 71
Ricketts, Kay 189
Rodrigues, Alexandra H. 239
Rootes, Neva 313
Rosa, Denise T. 149
Ross, Jylan 5
Ruiz, Anthony 316
Russell, Judy E. 255

S

Sabiston, Larry 236
Safko, Dorothy 250
Sanchez, Ipolita 226
Sappenfield, Royce W. 127
Scatterday, Blin B. 253
Schaible, Michael C. 208
Schanzenbach, Megan 241
Schowalter, Ruth E. 321
Schumaker, Joli 120

Scouten, Gary Lee 161
Seiter, Mary Alice 23
Selby, Jennie 192
Sellingsloh, Hulda K. 72
Shavender, Marilyn 308
Shlepr, Betty 181
Shuttleworth, William H. 9
Siedzik, Mildred J. 225
Smith, Catherine 260
Smith, Gloria R. 309
Smith, Michael Kirby 145
Smith, Norm 62
Smith, Roy A. 177
Smith, Virgilia A. 36
Soutra, Corinne 224
Spence, William R. 11
Starsiak, Roberta G. 232
Staudenraus, Jerry 302
Steele, Caroline 125
Stein, Marc B. 52
Stephens, B. Kay 171
Stepsay, Richard 8
Sterczala, Michael David 199
Stoermer, Darlene D. 323
Student, Lawrence D. 257
Swan, Kenneth 191

T

Takano Sliger, Ruth 166
Tambo, Josephine 298
Tatham, Eufemia 173
Taylor, Anthony 30
Taylor, Jewelean 273
Taylor, Nancy 162
Teixeira, Annette J. 295
Than, Waimar 205
Thompson, Elizabeth 22
Tokunaga Kus, Michiko 92
Tomkins, Sarah Beth 314
Tripodi, Tony 252
Tripp, Beck 45
Tucker, Robert P. 294
Tuttle, Sarah 304
Tyler, Lucille 16
Tyson, Wycliffe 129

U

Urseth, Mary Jo 85

V

Valnoha, Otto 50
Vanderleek, Maria 279
Varney, Jeff 278
Vaysman, Leonid 218
Versfelt, L. Janeene 134
Vigil, Eileen 148
Villanova, Rhonda C. 77
Violette-Hayden, Patsy 124
Voirol, Glenn 213
Vollaro, Jessica 31

W

Walker, Omar A. 108
Walsh, Derek 155
Warren, Constance 94
Warren, Melita 153
Washington, Ellery 262
Watt, Bill M. 186
Weiland, Ashley 227
Wenstad, Melvin Peter 297
Westbury, Shirley A. 319
Wilkerson, Joyce M. 276
Willey, Roger L. 299
William, Hugo T. 196
Williams, Carol 122
Williams, Chester 185
Williams, Curtis L. 18
Williams, Shirlene D. 117
Wilson, Ben, Jr. 178
Wilson, Leeland 51
Witt, Gladys R. 25
Wolfe, Billie L. 55
Wood, Virchel E. 81
Woolschlager, Laura T. 221
Word, Pat 107
Worley, Heather R. 197

Y

Yoder, Rebekah 325
Young, Sandra A. 164

Z

Zemp, LaWayne 293
Zimmerman, Shirley A. 115
Zoë, Shalom Christina 180
Zoller, Ollie V. 156